# RATIONALLY RIGHT

# RATIONALLY RIGHT

## An Explanation of
## the Conservative Paradigm

## Stephen R. Meyer

Beaver's Pond Press, Inc.
Edina, Minnesota

ISBN 1-931646-53-8

Library of Congress Catalog Number: 2002107469


Book design and typesetting: Mori Studio
Cover design: Mori Studio

Printed in the United States of America

First Printing: July 2002

06 05 04 03 02   6 5 4 3 2 1


Beaver's Pond Press, Inc.    5125 Danen's Drive
Edina, MN 55439-1465
(952) 829-8818
www.BeaversPondPress.com

To order, visit MidwestBookHouse.com or call 1-877-430-0044. Quantity discounts available.

# TABLE OF CONTENTS

# ACKNOWLEDGMENTS

I wish to thank my parents, Richard and Patricia Meyer, for my conservative upbringing and for reviewing this writing. I especially want to thank my wife, Debbie, and my sister, Barb Janas, for their support and direction. I would also like to thank my son Nick and my daughter Bridget for putting up with having to hear about this subject matter for the years it took me to finally complete this book. My sincere thanks to my editors, Krista Smith, Cindy Rodgers, and Jeri Youness. Ms. Smith accepted the unenviable task of putting my writing into a readable form. I also wish to thank Ms. Smith for arguing from the liberal position, which greatly helped in clarifying my thoughts.

I wish to thank the following three economists who, outside my family, had the greatest influence on my thinking: Milton Friedman, Thomas Sowell, and Walter Williams. Milton Friedman did a television series called *Free to Choose*, which aired on PBS back in my teenage years. *Free to Choose* introduced me to Thomas Sowell. The person who most reflects my train of thought in the conservative crowd is Walter Williams. Read anything from these three and I don't think you will be disappointed.

I wish to thank futurist and author Joel Barker for introducing me to the concept of paradigms, and author John Bradshaw for explaining the concept of dysfunction.

Although PBS is a government-supported entity, I would nevertheless like to thank PBS for airing some very interesting and thought-provoking television.

I wish to thank the many conservative talk-show hosts who supply information from the conservative point of view on both social and political issues. I would also like to thank *The Wall Street Journal* for publishing its mostly conservative editorial section, which often reminds me that conservatives have cohorts both here and around the world striving for the good of the people.

# NOTE TO READERS

One of the primary reasons I wrote this book was to try to influence non-conservative voters to be more open to the conservative political message. I also wanted to make the book interesting for conservatives, and to give conservative readers additional political food for thought.

Those of you in my first audience—non-conservatives—may find the ideas presented here difficult to accept. Mindsets are difficult to change. I know people who will vote for Democrats for the remainder of their lives because Franklin Roosevelt brought electricity to rural America. I would say that these voters are really stuck in their paradigm. (If you're not familiar with the concept, paradigms will be discussed in the first chapter.) I'm not belittling that mindset; if you lived and worked on a farm without the aid of electricity, I'm sure you would have been ecstatic when electricity finally arrived. But ecstatic enough to vote for Democrats for the remainder of your life?

You may think you are an open-minded person, but I'll guarantee you that the minute you read something in this book that violates one of your heartfelt political beliefs you will have emotionally quit reading. You may physically finish the book, but you will be reading it only to find additional information that violates your political paradigm and therefore offers further proof that these ideas are intellectually corrupt.

The fact that I wanted to try to reach two very different audiences left me in a dilemma. If I targeted the book too much at conservatives, then it would be too antagonistic for non-conservatives to read. If I presented the conservative paradigm in such a way as to be acceptable to non-conservatives, then the book would be of no interest to the conservative reader. I could have written more than one book on basically the same subject, but this was not an appealing option. The book is fairly short, and making it even shorter didn't seem like the right thing to do. I had one other thought.

The idea is this: I am asking you to skip, for some period of time, those chapters that you know will not fit into your political paradigm. Waiting a year to finish the book would be an acceptable amount of time.

What will be accomplished by waiting a year? I would like to sneak some conservative thoughts into your head and your heart, where they will hopefully find fruitful ground and grow. Once you have a better understanding of the conservative paradigm, you may start to notice things in the liberal paradigm that just don't seem right. At this point the liberal and conservative paradigms will begin a turf battle over your political heart and soul, but this turf battle will take time to be waged. If I overwhelm you with too much conservatism all at once, you're likely to flatly reject everything I say, and these new thoughts will never have a chance to take hold.

Within this year, I hope that you would search out other conservative writings, such as those of F. A. Hayek, Milton Friedman, Walter Williams, and Thomas Sowell. I also hope that you would seek out other conservative thought. You could actually even talk to a conservative. We conservatives may not be as approachable as we could be, but the conservatives I personally know are really nice people.

How do you go about waiting for a year? Lend the book to an unreliable friend who won't return it until asked. Lend the book to a friend who will lend it to other friends, and you won't be able to track it down for a year. Have your e-mail system, or a note in your planner, remind you to finish the book in a year. You could even do what I would do, which would be to put the book in a place I know I'd never forget, and it would take me a year to remember where that place was. Do anything, but don't read those chapters now.

I tried to order the book in such a way that the material that is least offensive to the liberal point of view is presented toward the beginning, and the material most offensive to the liberal paradigm in the later chapters. Among these less objectionable early chapters, however, is a chapter on Social Security. If you think Social Security is the greatest thing in the world, then please skip that chapter for now. If you are adamant in your defense of abortion rights, then please skip my chapter on abortion for now. I think you will be able to tell when you are nearing the point where your paradigm is sufficiently challenged. At that point, close the book and wait the required year to complete the reading.

Thank you for your patience and understanding.

*Stephen Meyer*

# INTRODUCTION

### The Story of Robin Hood

The classic tale of the legendary Robin Hood is the story of a man who lived in England during medieval times. Robin Hood, a member of the English aristocracy, was forced from his comfortable lifestyle because of his opposition to the government of Prince John. Robin joined a marauding band of thieves living in the inhospitable Sherwood Forest. These good-hearted thieves stole from the idle rich and distributed the stolen riches to the poor.

The story of Robin Hood warms liberal hearts, and in the spirit of Robin Hood, the liberal goes forth in good conscience to tax the rich and redistribute the wealth to the poor, the suffering, and the infirm.

I, on the other hand, see the story of the legendary Robin Hood as a classic conservative tale. Robin Hood and his band of merry men were stealing from the rich, but it was the rich who had obtained their ill-gotten wealth from taxing the peasants. What Robin Hood and his men were doing was staging a guerrilla war from Sherwood Forest against the government of the evil Prince John. Prince John and his cohort, the Sheriff of Nottingham, were the leaders of the English government while King Richard the Lionhearted was off fighting in the Crusades. The government of Prince John levied inordinately high taxes on the peasants, and used brutal means to collect the taxes. Much of this wealth went straight into the pockets of Prince John and his political followers.

In the conservative paradigm it is believed that intrusive governments remove wealth from the people and transfer this wealth to wasteful bureaucracies and others who are not poor, and in so doing lower the people's standard of living. We, of the conservative paradigm, would like to emulate Robin Hood in fighting for the people and against big and intrusive government.

In this book I compare liberal and conservative positions on a variety of significant political issues. Common language is defined, hopefully enabling conservatives and non-conservatives to discuss politics from common ground. The largest part of the book addresses taxes and the inconceivable size of our government. The book concludes with a strategy to bring other caring voters into the progressive conservative political paradigm.

# CHAPTER ONE

# PARADIGMS

From the interpretation of the story of Robin Hood in the introductory chapter, you can see that there is a significant difference between liberal and conservative views. For the most part, liberals and conservatives want the same things: world peace, affordable housing, less poverty, a good education system, less crime, a healthy and wealthy population, a safe environment, and so on. Where liberals and conservatives differ is on how these results are to be achieved, and whether these results can be achieved. But why do the liberals and conservatives have such differing views of the world?

I have always liked to discuss politics, and I have always taken the conservative position. In my political discussions I've found it frustrating to talk politics with a non-conservative person and not to be able to convince that person of my way of thinking. It seemed that my political discussions would turn into political arguments. These political arguments would get louder and louder, until the argument would finally end with the non-conservative more hardened in his or her liberal view than when we first started the discussion. Not exactly the outcome I had in mind at the beginning of the political discussion.

There were years of this frustration before I heard futurist Joel Barker address the concept of paradigms. (To review Barker's very interesting work, please read *Discovering the Future: The Business of Paradigms*.) I suddenly realized that I had been arguing my position from within my conservative political paradigm, while my non-conservative opponent had been arguing his or her position from within the liberal political paradigm. There was no way the argument could end with either of us changing our minds because we would never be able to change the other's political paradigm.

The concept of paradigms has been around for some time now, and many of you may be familiar with it already. For those of you who are not familiar with paradigms, the following is my attempt at an explanation.

What is a paradigm? A paradigm is the way an object or idea is perceived. A paradigm could be called a mindset.

You may not even be able to discuss a new concept without an education in the language involved in the paradigm. Take the computer, for example. There are words that didn't even exist prior to the computer. Who ever heard of downloads, RAM, online, offline, baud rates, and so on? When computer people discuss computers, they could be speaking a foreign language as far as I'm concerned. The computer people are in their own paradigm. They understand this computer language, and will not even discuss computers technically with those of us who don't understand this computer language. To technically discuss computers with people who are not technically knowledgeable about computers would be a waste of the computer people's time. We non-computer people are not in the computer people's paradigm.

Being in different paradigms is somewhat like two people speaking different languages. When speaking different languages, however, you are aware that the other person probably doesn't understand what you are saying. When you are in different paradigms, you may not even realize that you are speaking languages with different meanings—such as when I entered into my previously mentioned political discussions.

One of my favorite examples of a paradigm is Joel Barker's story of the Swiss watch industry. After World War II, the Swiss dominated the watch industry. A forward-looking consortium of Swiss watch companies pooled their resources to set up a research and development group to ensure that they maintained the Swiss technological superiority and retained their dominant market position. This Swiss research team developed a new product. The new watch was inexpensive to manufacture, and it kept perfect time. The team brought this new quartz watch to the leaders of the consortium.

You can guess—or perhaps you know—the consortium leaders' reaction. The consortium leaders knew about the tiny springs and gears and how they all worked together in their engineered masterpieces. In the consortium leaders' paradigm, watches had to have gears and springs, and in this new watch there was not a spring or gear to be found. The leaders saw the new watch with this new quartz technology and instructed the research team to come up with something new and different that used gears and springs.

The disappointed research team that had developed the technology brought the new quartz watch to an industry trade show. Some Japanese businesspeople saw the watch at the trade show and realized the possibilities of the new design. The Japanese eventually launched a hugely successful watch business based on this quartz technology.

What was the watch consortium leaders' problem? The answer is that the quartz watch was a paradigm shift. The consortium leaders had the mindset that watches had to have gears and springs. The leaders probably didn't understand how the quartz watch worked. The leaders had a vested interest in keeping the watch industry from changing. But it really didn't matter what the leaders thought. The paradigm existed. The world of watches had changed. They did not understand that their products made of gears and springs had just become obsolete, and it cost the Swiss watch industry dearly.

The reason I use this Swiss watch example is because it highlights how people can behave. I personally find the consortium leaders' reaction a bit scary. The design team had come up with exactly what the leaders had requested at the outset, which was a technical breakthrough that would maintain the Swiss watch industry's position as market leader.

These Swiss business leaders were probably extremely intelligent, hard working, and well educated. The leaders were titans of industry and prominent in their field. Yet they couldn't make the correct business decision because they were so locked into their spring-and-gear paradigm.

You could say that finding out about paradigms was a paradigm shift for me. When I applied the concept of paradigms to politics, it made sense why changing others' political mindsets was so difficult.

Although I have never heard Milton Freedman speak of paradigms, I believe he has the best explanation for the formation of the liberal and conservative paradigms. My summary of Friedman's ideas follows in the next two paragraphs.

The liberal economic paradigm is based on the liberal view that capitalism failed in the late 1920s. The failure was expressed in the stock market collapse, which was the start of the Great Depression. The Great Depression led to a global downturn, which gave rise to German Nazism, which eventually led to World War II. In the liberal paradigm, government participation in the economy and society is not only preferred, but also necessary to prevent disasters such as the Great Depression.

The conservative economic paradigm is based on the conservative view that the cause of the Great Depression was not the failure of the marketplace, but the failure of the government-controlled monetary system. Overspeculation led to a stock market sell-off, which contracted the amount of money in circulation. The government (through delegation to the Federal Reserve) failed to inject money into the economy after the market crash, which led to bank failures, which caused an even greater shrinkage of the money supply, which eventually caused the economy to implode. The lack of money in our free-market system led to the Great Depression. The Great Depression led to a global downturn, which gave rise to German Nazism, which eventually led to World War II. In the conservative paradigm, societies with limited but competent governments and free-market economic systems create the most wealth and have populations with the highest standards of living.

To the liberal, the capitalist system failed and the result of this failure was the Great Depression. To the conservative, the government failed in its responsibility to adequately supply our free-market economy with money, causing the Great Depression. Two very different views of the same problem. Two very different conclusions drawn from the same event. Two very different paradigms.

In the table below, I list the main tenets of the two opposing political paradigms. Most people do not fall consistently into the same column on every issue, but the comparisons drawn here illustrate some of the basic differences between the traditional liberal and conservative paradigms. The list of the conservative positions are my positions; I have sought others' help in identifying some of the liberal positions.

| THE LIBERAL PARADIGM | THE CONSERVATIVE PARADIGM |
|---|---|
| The government is a benevolent entity. | Some government is necessary, but too much government leads to loss of freedom. |
| It is acceptable, and oftentimes desirable, to forcibly take wealth from some to give to others through taxation. | It is unjust to forcibly take wealth from some to give to others through taxation. |
| Government running of services such as the postal service and the public school system is desirable. | Government running of anything is not desirable. The government should become involved only if there is no other alternative. |
| Public institutions are good for everyone. | Government institutions may be good, but only market competition can guarantee that institutions will be good. |
| Freedom of speech is applicable to all speech except speech that poses a physical danger to others (such as falsely yelling "Fire!" in a crowded auditorium) and religious speech in public schools or at government-sponsored events. | Freedom of speech, as described in the Constitution, protects only political speech. Other speech, such as obscene speech, has no constitutional protection. |
| Separation of church and state means that the state should be entirely non-religious. | Separation of church and state means that there should be no official state church. |
| Government should participate in the planning and financing of promising industries. | Business and state should be separate (in much the same way liberals view the separation of church and state). |

| | |
|---|---|
| Industry should be regulated by government. | Free markets operate most efficiently and create the greatest wealth. |
| The government should grant workers rights such as favorable union rights, minimum wage laws, mandated leave requirements, and so on. | Having a strong economy that increases the demand—and therefore the value—of workers best preserves workers' rights. |
| The country's economic policies should be aimed at creating jobs. | The country's economic policies should be aimed at creating wealth. |
| Military spending is always too great, and every effort should be made to prevent wars by dialogue. | Every cent of military spending to prevent wars is money well spent. |
| The capitalist economic system cannot adequately address issues of pollution, environmental degradation, and the disappearance of species because the time horizons involved are too long and it is too difficult to assign an economic value to public goods that will be enjoyed by future generations. | The government should play a role in ensuring that its citizens have clean air and water, and that unique park areas are preserved as public property; however, individuals' constitutional rights should not be trampled in the name of environmental concerns. |
| Global warming is a critical environmental problem that will require extensive government involvement to address. | Mankind's influence on possible global warming is unproven. No new taxes should be levied in the name of protecting the global environment. |
| Guns are more likely to fall into the hands of criminals or be involved in accidental shootings than they are to provide protection from crime. The constitutional right to bear arms was intended primarily to support the establishment of a militia, which is no longer a relevant issue. | Law-abiding citizens should be allowed to own firearms and use them in self-defense. |
| Society should attempt to right past injustices by granting privileges based on such criteria as race and gender. | No special privileges should be given to any group. |
| Welfare provides a safety net for the unfortunate, allowing them to become contributing members of society again. | Welfare promotes dependency on the government. |
| Criminals should be rehabilitated. | Criminals should be kept out of society. |

It is common to think of the political spectrum as a line with liberals to the left and conservatives at the right (see illustration below). At the extreme left of this line would be socialism and communism; to the extreme right, fascism, theocracy, and dictatorship. I cannot find a place for myself on this line, and I would guess most readers cannot find a place for themselves. I am not at all politically in favor of fascism, theocracy, or dictatorships. I am equally not in favor of socialism or communism. That would leave me in the middle, where I would be depicted as being somewhat liberal and somewhat conservative, which is an incorrect depiction of my political stance.

In the conservative paradigm, the political spectrum is also represented by a line, but to the right is freedom and liberty and to the left is serfdom and repression. This conservative depiction moves fascism, theocracies, and dictatorships off to the left along with their fellow freedom-restricting political systems of communism and socialism. In this depiction, I am able to place myself to the far right, which correctly depicts my political stance.

| | |
|---|---|
| Socialism | Theocracy<br>Fascism |
| Communism | Dictatorship |

←Liberalism                                                  Conservatism→

Common Depiction of Political Continuum

| | |
|---|---|
| Theocracies | |
| Socialism | |
| Communism | |
| Fascism | US Constitutional Republic |
| Dictatorships | as Originally Established |

←Serfdom, Repression                          Liberty, Freedom→
                                               Modern Conservatism→

Conservative Depiction of Political Continuum

# CHAPTER TWO

# TOTAL COST AND EXPERIMENTATION

In addition to the previously mentioned concept of paradigms, I would like to introduce the concepts of total cost and experimentation before further pursuing the political discussions.

First, a few words about experimentation. The only way I know to obtain indisputable answers to multivariable questions is to run experiments and observe the results of the experiments. Historically, conducting large-scale experiments has been a costly endeavor. However, a more efficient way of running experiments, known as fractional experimentation, has recently emerged. (This is a fairly old concept that was adopted and refined by Japanese businesses. In Japan it is known as the Taguchi method of experimentation.) Fractional experimentation limits the number of experiments that need to be conducted in order to derive an answer to a question. If politicians understood the benefits of fractional experimentation, they could use experimental data to optimize government.

Here is an example. Say you wanted to maximize government revenue. You could raise income taxes, but we know from history that raising taxes causes disincentive to work, so the tax increase might actually result in less revenue being collected. You could raise capital gains taxes, but we know from experience that a higher capital gains tax reduces activity in capital markets, so the tax increase may or may not result in increased revenues. You could cut both taxes, or raise one tax and lower the other. Perhaps the effect would be different in different parts of the country. Perhaps there are other significant factors, such as how people view the predictability of tax rates. By now, with all of these options, you have a fairly complicated problem. To solve this, I would call in a designer of experiments. The designer could develop a fractional experiment that would yield much meaningful information. Further fractional experimental iterations might be needed to arrive at the ultimate answer, but after one experimental run, a great deal of useful information would have been produced. I would actually like to see this experiment undertaken.

The second concept, total cost, is the idea of looking at an action in terms of the total cost incurred as a result of the action—both the initial cost and the long-term cost.

In the liberal paradigm, government plays many vital roles and runs many vital programs. In the conservative paradigm, many of these government programs are not vital and are not cost effective. Where the conservative and liberal paradigms differ is in the benefit derived from the resources spent on a government program. The resources spent on the government program should be examined from the standpoint of total cost.

Let's say, for example, that you buy a $20,000 car at the same time your neighbor purchases a $25,000 car. Over the next few years, your car is in and out of the repair shop and it ends up costing you $2,000 a year in repairs during the first three years of ownership. You notice that your neighbor's more expensive car is never in the shop and that the neighbor has not spent any money on repairing the $25,000 car. You add up the cost of repair and add it to the purchase price of the car, and you realize that you actually spent more on your car in total than your neighbor did on the more expensive car. Your total cost in this example was $26,000, while your neighbor's total cost was $25,000.

Let's take this concept further. In addition to the purchase price of the car, you will also have the expense of fuel, maintenance, insurance, taxes, and depreciation. If you buy a poor-quality car that requires frequent repairs and has poor resale value, the total cost may end up being much more than the total cost of a car that doesn't need repair and has high resale value. Another cost that should be included in the discussion is the car's ability to keep you safe. Medical costs could be by far your greatest expense if you purchased an unsafe vehicle and you were involved in an accident.

With many political issues, the only costs that are taken into account are the first costs. Two examples are welfare and defense spending. What is the cost of welfare? We can look at the budget numbers and find a cost. The problem is that this is not the total cost of welfare, but only the first cost. We do not look at the additional cost to the welfare recipient of not gaining work experience. We do not look at the cost to taxpayers of not having the tax money that was taken from them to pay for the welfare program. We don't question the moral cost of a person being idle, or the cost to the welfare recipient's children of seeing parents who are not contributing to society. The list of costs goes on and on, but you will never hear a pro-welfare politician address these additional costs. The problem is that these additional costs exceed the first costs of the welfare program by a huge margin.

Many conservative politicians intuitively recognize the high total cost of welfare but are not able to articulate their objections in these terms because they are unfamiliar with this concept of total cost. As a result, they attack the welfare program and end up appearing as though they oppose helping the poor. Political opponents jump right in to take political advantage.

By using the concept of total cost, the conservative can argue not against the first cost, but against the huge total cost of maintaining our present welfare system—the cost to our society as well as the personal cost to the welfare recipient. We conservatives are not against helping the poor; we just know that the huge total cost to the welfare recipient is more than anyone should have to bear.

Conversely, liberals frequently attack defense spending as an un- necessary government expense, whereas in the conservative paradigm, having a strong military discourages our enemies from waging war against us. The liberals look only at the first cost of defense spending, while the conservatives look at the total cost of war. What is the total cost of war? What is the cost of the lives that are lost? What is the cost of losing a parent, a child, or a sibling? What is the cost to those who survive, but who are physically or emotionally damaged for life? What is the cost of the lost loves, and the families that are ruined? What is the cost of the national treasures that are destroyed or irreparably damaged? What are the environmental costs? The cost of war is incalculable, but the liberal does not consider this huge total cost when cutting defense spending. The September 11, 2001, terrorist attacks also highlighted this total cost concept. What was the total cost of failing to prevent this attack?

The concept of total cost was developed by businesses to help them maintain a competitive cost advantage over other businesses. Politicians rarely examine total cost. Politicians do not have to worry about costs in the same way a competitive business has to because the government has no competition. This lack of concern about cost and the government's ability to force funds from taxpayers has caused the government to become a very large entity.

# CHAPTER THREE

# THE SIZE OF THE UNITED STATES GOVERNMENT

In the conservative paradigm, government action always comes with a cost. In the conservative paradigm, government should act only where no market exists or where the action is a constitutional mandate of the government. In the liberal paradigm, government can never get too big because there is always someone else the government can help or some other problem the government can solve. This view has caused our government to become huge.

Just how large is our federal government? I thought it would be interesting to try to come up with something with which to compare the size of the government. The first thing I tried to compare to the government's size was my salary. I calculated how long my salary would finance the federal budget. I'm sorry to report that my salary would finance the government for less than a second. I tried comparing the federal budget to sports stars' salaries that run into the millions, but their salaries would only finance the federal government for a matter of minutes. Bill Gates—the founder of Microsoft, the richest person in America, and the holder of billions of dollars worth of stock—could finance the federal government for a little over a week. I had to think bigger.

I believe things that happen during a person's late teenage years make a lasting impression. I turned eighteen in 1974. It was the height of the first energy crisis. I bought the story of ever-increasing oil prices. In the late 1970s I even quit college and started a project to figure out how to burn wood more efficiently during a subsequent energy crisis. I was waiting for the predicted $60-per-barrel oil prices. Now it's more than two decades later, and even with inflation we have not seen $50-per-barrel oil, let alone $60-per-barrel oil.

In the 1970s, people were concerned about how energy costs were forever going to change their lives. Here were a bunch of rich sheiks who had nothing to do all day but watch the pumping of oil—which American and other Western oil companies had discovered—and collect the resulting flow of money. They had, in our collective eyes, our future controlled. The Organization of Petroleum Exporting Countries (OPEC) controlled the production rate of the majority of the world's exportable oil, and by changing their production levels, OPEC members could drive the price of oil to whatever level they desired.

Before I continue, I would like to ask you a question. Which of the following time frames is closest to how long one day of oil revenue from OPEC would fund the federal government? I'll give you some hints. OPEC produces somewhere around 25 million barrels of oil per day, and there are 42 gallons in a barrel of oil.

    A.  1 year

    B.  4 months

    C.  1 month

    D.  1 week

    E.  2 days

    F.  1 hour

OPEC is the largest producer of oil in the world, and oil is one of the world's biggest businesses. The price of oil and OPEC production levels are variable. The following numbers are taken from the December 31, 2001, issue of *The Wall Street Journal* and exclude Iraq. The article said that OPEC collected $206.6 billion in oil revenues in 2001.

The following comparison uses just the receipts of the federal government. The numbers do not include state and local government receipts, nor do they represent the total financial impact of the federal government.

As mentioned in the above question, OPEC produced about 25 million barrels of oil per day in 2001. The revenue produced by this quantity of oil was $564,657,535 per day (about $565 million) in 2001. In 2001 the federal government's annual receipts were $1,991,500,000,000 ($1 trillion, 991.5 billion; see Appendix), which is approximately $5,456,000,000 ($5.456 billion) per day, based on a 365-day year. (I put all the zeros in just in case you want to double-check my math.) Dividing $5.456 billion of government spending per day in 2001 by the $565 million of OPEC revenue generated each day in 2001—or dividing the 2001 $1.9915 trillion in annual federal receipts by OPEC's 2001 revenue of $206.6 billion—gives you about 9.6.

So if you answered F to the previous question, you would have been correct. The federal government's 2001 receipts were about nine times greater than the revenue OPEC collected in 2001. The huge sum of money that OPEC generates each day would finance our government for about two and a half hours out of every twenty-four-hour day, or about fifty minutes out of an eight-hour day. Another way of looking at this would be to say that OPEC would need to produce oil for over nine days to match one day of federal government revenue.

Can you imagine? Our federal government is nine times bigger than OPEC! All those supertankers, pipelines, oil wells, and refineries—and our government was nine times bigger than OPEC in 2001. I find this truly amazing. Nine times bigger than OPEC. If a day begins at midnight, by 3.00 A.M., our federal government would have spent all the revenue produced by OPEC during a full day of pumping oil. In an eight-hour day, starting at 8:00 A.M., the government would have spent all of OPEC's revenues by 8:50 A.M.

The United States is prepared to go to war in the Middle East at the slightest hint of disruption to the flow of oil, yet our federal government alone is more than nine times larger than OPEC. We think of OPEC as being a huge financial force, but OPEC is not even in the big leagues.

To further compare spending on oil and spending on government let us look at the U.S. daily oil consumption of imported oil and federal government revenue. The U.S. consumes about 19 million barrels of oil a day; 60 percent of this oil is imported, which leaves us using 11.4 million barrels of imported oil per day. Multiplying 11.4 million barrels of oil by a cost of $25 per barrel yields a daily expenditure of $285,000,000 ($285 million). The spending on imported oil equals about 5.2 percent of the daily revenue taken by our federal government (the federal government collects about $19 from taxpayers in the same period of time that our foreign suppliers of oil collect $1 from American oil consumers).

Another interesting comparison came to mind when I was preparing the table in the appendix showing the 2001 federal government revenue and spending. The interest payment on our national debt last year was $206.2 billion, which almost matched the $206.6 billion in 2001 OPEC revenues. We are paying almost twice as much on federal debt interest payments as we are spending on imported oil ($206.4 billion in debt service versus $104 billion spent on imported oil).

This huge government size is not restricted to just tax collection. I was reading the April 2002 edition of the *National Geographic*, which has a feature article called *Ask Us*. The article stated that nearly one-third of all U.S. land is under federal government control. Conservatives look at the government as a huge business with the ability to force its customers to pay for the business's products and services. This huge business owns nearly one-third of all of the land in the United States and has an operating budget of over $2 trillion.

How is our government able to collect such large sums of money and control so much wealth? One way to do this is to disguise how much wealth the government takes. The amount of money taxpayers are actually forced to pay to the government is very well disguised, so as not to reveal the true amount of money the government consumes.

CHAPTER FOUR

# GENERAL TAXATION

In the conservative paradigm, taxes are the vehicle that the government uses to extract wealth from the wealth-producing free market. The conservative paradigm recognizes that some of this taxation of the free market supports necessary government activities, but much tax revenue is taken for unnecessary and oftentimes harmful government activities.

I like to compare the government to a casino. The first rule of casinos is that they take their earnings from the winners. This strategy of taking earnings from just the winners allows everyone to be fairly happy. The bettors who lose feel as though they should have lost their money. They knowingly made a wager and they lost; there are no hard feelings. The winners are happy because they have won. They may not have won as much as they could have if the casino hadn't taken some of their winnings, but they are still ahead. This is very similar to the way in which the government sets tax policy.

The government taxes the winners of our society at extremely high levels. The current data suggests that the top 5 percent of taxpayers pay approximately 50 percent of all income taxes, and the top 50 percent of taxpayers pay virtually all of the income tax. The high earners complain of the high rates, but they are still doing well, so the voters and politicians keep their tax rates high. (Just for clarification, I am not including the 6.2 percent Social Security tax or the 1.45 percent Medicare tax—applied to both employee and employer—in the discussion on income taxes. I do this even though Social Security and Medicare taxes are, in my view, income taxes.)

The second rule of betting establishments is to hide the fact that the house is taking money. A casino does this by setting the odds in its favor. At a betting establishment, the bettor thinks he or she is making an even-money bet, but the casino will have slightly better odds. The bettors don't realize that they are losing more often than they would have if the odds were even. Likewise, tax policy is written to hide taxes. A prime example of a hidden tax is the employer's payment of half of the employee's Social Security and Medicare taxes.

These Social Security and Medicare taxes that the employer pays are really taxes on the wages earned, but they are hidden from the wage earner. The employee's wages are lower than they would be without the tax. Self-employed people see this huge tax burden because they have to pay both the employer's half and the employee's half of the Social Security and Medicare taxes. This tax rate of 15.3 percent is obvious to these people, and they justly complain loudly. If you have ever wondered why small businesspeople hate big government, part of the reason is that they see the total cost of the Social Security and Medicare system. The Social Security program looks much better than it would if people realized how much their employer was contributing to the program.

Another way the government hides the size of tax payments is to withhold the taxes from the taxpayer's paycheck. You lose the concept of how much you are paying because the money for taxes disappears before you are even able to take control of it. If you had to write a check to the government every time you received a paycheck, you would be much more aware of what you are paying to the government in taxes. As the system is set up, most taxpayers are only concerned about whether they get money back when they file their annual tax returns in the spring.

Casinos also make some money by offering complicated games. You lose money while you are trying to figure the game out. Taxes are extremely complicated. You lose tax money while trying to figure out the tax system or by paying a tax preparer who (you hope) has the tax system figured out.

The government has in its favor one other trick that the casinos cannot duplicate. This trick is inflation. Inflation occurs when the overall cost of goods and services increase without an increase in real value. If only income taxes are included, the income tax system is progressive. As your earnings rise, the inflation that caused your earning increase also increases your tax liability.

Let's use a simple example that doesn't take deductions into account. In this example, you have taxable income of $60,000, the inflation rate is 5 percent, and the tax rate on the first $45,200 is 15 percent. The tax rate on the remainder is 27.5 percent. Your income tax this year would then be $10,850. If your wages just keep pace with inflation, then your next year's taxable income becomes $63,000, and your income taxes would be $11,675. Because you are paying the second-year tax with inflated dollars, the income tax, using inflation-adjusted numbers, would be $11,119—an increase of $319. No one in government had to vote to increase your income tax by $319. The income tax increase was automatic and caused by inflation.

I group taxes into two categories: hidden and non-hidden. The non-hidden taxes are those that you see and know you are paying. These would include sales taxes, income taxes, part of your Social Security tax, property taxes, and so on. The hidden taxes are those that you don't see and you are unaware that you are paying. Examples of these taxes are your employer's half of the Social Security tax, government regulations that drive up the cost of the products and services that you purchase, business taxes, unemployment taxes, government-mandated import or export tariffs, minimum wage laws, tax increases owing to inflation, lottery ticket costs, and so on.

Any fair tax system should have the following features:

- Tax rates, both marginal and overall, should be as low as possible to maximize the incentives to work and invest.
- The tax system should be simple and understandable, and taxes should not be hidden.

- The tax system should not tax people of lower incomes at a higher rate than those who have higher incomes.

- The tax system should consider wealth and not just income when determining who should be taxed. The current discussion on taxes confuses wealth and income by implying that those with high taxable incomes are rich and those with low taxable incomes are poor (to be discussed in detail in Chapter Five).

Our present system fails to meet all of these criteria.

How does our present system cause disincentive to work and invest? Pretend you are a carpenter. It's December, and up to this point you and your spouse have made $60,000 this year. A prospective client calls about a job. You value your skills at $20 per hour. You take a look at the job and determine that it will take 80 hours of your time. You calculate how much you will charge—80 hours times $20 per hour yields $1,600. Now you figure in the taxes that will have to be paid. If you calculate 27.5 percent federal tax, a combined 15.3 percent Social Security and Medicare tax, and let's say a 7.2 percent state income tax, the total tax adds up to 50 percent. You take the $1,600 and multiply it by two to pay your wages plus the taxes, and this comes to a total of $3,200. The customer receiving the bid roughly calculates that you will be receiving $40 per hour and politely declines the bid.

Everyone loses in this example. The potential customer will have to take some other action or not have the work done at all. The carpenter realizes no new income. The government gets 50 percent of nothing. No tax system should have a marginal tax rate approaching anywhere near the 50 percent level.

In the conservative paradigm, most business taxes are really hidden taxes. Businesses really don't care what the tax rate is as long as all of their competitors pay the same tax. Taxes are the same to a business as any other cost. The business will include the tax cost as part of the price of the product or service being sold. Business A objects when Business B gets a lower tax rate, putting A at a competitive disadvantage. But as long as A's costs are the same as B's, A will be able to pass the cost of the tax on to its customers. When you purchase a new car, you are also purchasing the business taxes that were paid in producing the car, such as the employer's half of the Social Security tax and the company's income tax. The following isn't exactly related to the discussion on business taxes, but in my home state, we then also pay a 6.5 percent sales tax on the price of the car—we even have to pay this sales tax on used cars regardless of the number of times the used car is sold. This tax applied to used cars really irritates me.

If conservative proposals are made to reduce business taxes, the first thing you hear from liberal politicians is that big businesses, which are making billions and billions of dollars, are getting tax breaks. The conservatives run for cover. The conservatives should stand and fight. Businesses don't pay taxes; their customers pay the taxes. The business is just the tax collector. Business taxes are just hidden taxes on consumers, consumers who may be poor and who can ill afford to pay this extra hidden tax. The government's ability to hide its revenue-generation methods is one of the reasons it has grown to be nine times bigger than OPEC.

There is another tax item that should be discussed while we are still addressing business taxes. Many schools are financed through property taxes. People vote in local referendums to increase property taxes to fund additional school spending. If the referendum passes, then the businesses within that school district—which already pay significant property taxes—face increased taxes without having any ability to vote on the increase. Is this fair?

The tax system is not simple and understandable, and many taxes are hidden. If you do your own taxes, you already realize that the tax system is not simple and understandable. If you don't do your own taxes, you should, just to get an understanding of how complex the process is. The more income you have and the more varied your business life is, the more complicated the tax system becomes. This is one of my biggest complaints of the tax system. Life is complicated enough without having to have such a complicated tax system. People and businesses spend what should be productive time trying to figure out ways to comply with the tax system and to legally minimize their taxation.

The third item is truly astonishing to me. In both the conservative and liberal paradigms, tax rates for people with less income should be lower or equal to the tax rates of higher-income people. If the Social Security tax is considered, however, the marginal tax rate is often much lower on the next dollar of income for the higher-income people. In my example above, the tax rate on the carpenter's next dollar of income was 50 percent. This rate is higher than that of a person whose income is much higher, owing to the fact that the Social Security tax is eliminated for earnings above $84,900 (the limit for 2002; the limit will continue to rise in the future). Those people who earn salaries approaching the $84,900 Social Security limit—and especially two-wage families—pay the highest marginal tax.

Our tax system really hits dual-wage-earning families. The second income of a two-income family will be taxed at the minimum of the highest tax rate of the first income, and will still be taxed for Social Security if the individual's income is less than the $84,900 Social Security limit.

The conservative paradigm recognizes that we live in a dynamic world. If one thing changes, then other things will be affected by the change. Often government action is viewed statically, and a change will be made with the assumption that it will not affect anything else. An example of this is tax rate changes. If government revenue is inadequate, then in a static world you would raise tax rates and government revenue would increase. In a dynamic world, an increase in taxes may or may not increase government revenues. The prime example of this idea in action is the reduction in high marginal tax rates that both Presidents Kennedy and Reagan implemented. The lower marginal tax rates led to increases in government revenue. Coupled with this idea of a dynamic world, we conservatives also believe that if you tax something you get less of it.

This brings me to an idea that I refer to as the negative employment effect of a free-market economy naturally adjusting to minimize taxation. My hypothesis is that a free-market economy will adjust to minimize total taxes. I have read many stories about how we are losing the middle class. You hear over and over from the media how the gap between the rich and the poor is widening and how there are fewer jobs for people in the middle. It appears to me that this lack of job creation or outright job loss is what you would expect given the tax rates. If your income is in a range where it is taxed by fairly high federal income taxes, the employee's and the employer's portion of the Social Security and Medicare taxes, and your state income tax, you pay very high marginal tax rates. You may not realize that your labor is carrying such a high tax burden because your employer is paying part of the tax, but your labor is carrying this high tax burden, nevertheless. Free markets will work against paying all of this tax. These high marginal tax rates will lead to the unintended consequence of having fewer jobs available in these salary ranges.

This high marginal tax rate also provides a negative work incentive. It is hard to find people to work overtime, even though they are paid at a pay rate of 150 percent of their normal wage. People compare their checks without overtime to their checks with overtime, and find that the hourly rate is approximately the same. The person who has worked the additional overtime is being taxed at this very high marginal tax rate.

I don't like hidden taxes, especially hidden employment taxes. Employees tend to think that their employer is cheating them when they see that their take-home pay is far less than the wealth they are creating for their employer.

A business will hire you for one and only one reason: the business wants to make money off of your labor. When you are hired for a job, your wage is only a part of the labor cost to the employer. The employer will have additional costs such as unemployment insurance taxes and the employer's share of the Social Security tax. The employer will pay for any fringe benefits, such as medical insurance, and the cost of non-working time, such as paid vacation, sick leave or maternity leave, and holiday pay. The employer will also have administrative costs involved with your employment, such as government-mandated training and on-the-job training, as well as other miscellaneous costs.

Let's take a simple example. An employer looks at a job and calculates what he or she can afford to pay for that job. Let's assume that the company can break even by paying $25 per hour for a given job. If the company's actual cost of employing someone is less than $25 per hour, it will make money; if it's more than $25 per hour, the company will lose money.

The employer wants to make $3 per hour off of your labor, so the money the employer is willing to budget for this job is $22 per hour for the total cost of your labor. Of this $22, what will you see as a wage? Assuming that you are actually at work for 90 percent of the time (ten paid holidays and ten paid vacation days per year, and a few days of paid sick leave), your employer will pay you $20 per hour for all payable hours in order to meet the $22 per hour that you are actually at work producing wealth for your employer. If the government unemployment insurance rate is 2 percent, the employer's part of the Social Security and Medicare tax is 7.65 percent, and other employee costs add up to $3 per hour, I calculate a wage of $15.50 [$15.50 + 2 percent unemployment tax ($15.50 x .02 = $.31) + 7.65 percent employer's portion of the Medicare and Social Security tax ($15.50 x .0765 = $1.19) + $3.00 in fringe benefits = $20.00]. The $15.50 wage is reduced by state and federal income taxes (let's say 20 percent total) and by the employee's half of the Social Security tax, yielding a take-home pay of $11.21 per hour [$15.50 - 20 percent income tax ($15.50 x .2 = $3.10) - 7.65 percent Social Security and Medicare taxes ($15.50 x .0765 = $1.19); $15.50 - $3.10 - $1.19 = $11.21].

Who does the employee blame when he or she sees only $11.21 per hour of the $25 per hour that the employee is creating in wealth? Knowledgeable employees blame the government. The not-so-knowledgeable blame the business. The truly bright quit and try to generate income that qualifies as capital gains, which is taxed at a lower rate and not taxed for Social Security.

There is one more item that I believe falls under the tax heading. As mentioned earlier, the top 5 percent of taxpayers pay 50 percent of the total income taxes, and the top 50 percent of taxpayers pay virtually all of the income tax. I've stated previously that incomes that pay the 27.5 percent federal tax rate and still pay Social Security taxes—such as second incomes in a two-income household—carry very high tax burdens. It is my belief, though, that there are two groups with even higher tax burdens than the groups earning high and second incomes.

I consider any government action that causes you financial loss—

either by actively taking your wealth through taxes or by preventing you from gaining wealth—as a form of taxation. Thus, the two highest taxed groups are the people whose skills are not worth the minimum wage, and young people who are not allowed to work because of their age. By law, young people cannot even be hired. Their tax rate is in essence so high that no one can even employ them. And this high rate is only the first cost. The total cost is even higher. They fail to gain work experience that will make them more valuable employees later, and they may even be forced into illegal employment, such as the drug trade, to meet their financial needs or wants. I do not even know how to try to put a tax burden on this situation, but it is extremely high, extremely unjust, and in need of change.

One more point while we're on the subject. The latest government movement is to force people off welfare and into jobs. Although conservatives are strong proponents of the value of work, we believe that this welfare reform effort could have unintended negative consequences if it is not accompanied by a loosening of labor-market restrictions. If there are restrictions on employment, such as the minimum wage and minimum age requirements, a real problem will be encountered by people whose skills are not worth the existing minimum wage or who are not old enough to legally hold a job. Picture yourself, for example, as a twelve-year-old child of a single mother who has just run out of welfare benefits. If the neighborhood crack house had a job available for a lookout, the temptation to take that job would be very high.

The conservative position should be to eliminate all the taxes, both hidden and non-hidden, on these low-income people. A low tax, or preferably no tax, on low incomes would build a vibrant economy, where none presently exists, among the poor. There would be learning instead of personal stagnation, hope instead of despair, personal responsibility instead of abdication of personal responsibility. Wealth would be created instead of consumed. I believe these work restrictions must be removed before welfare can be eliminated. I can think of no worse situation than being completely excluded from the labor market because of age or limited ability. I believe the only other option for these people is crime—either illegal employment or out-and-out crime.

# CHAPTER FIVE

# TAXES ON THE MIDDLE CLASS AND WORKING POOR

The vast majority of middle-income workers and the working poor are not represented by anyone in the media or in politics. The major media outlets and the liberal wing of the Democratic Party represent the welfare points of view. Business publications and the wealthy wings of both political parties represent the wealthy views.

You may be taken aback by my reference to the wealthy of both political parties. The popular political paradigm holds that the wealthy are all conservatives. There is no way to know exactly what a voter's wealth is, since our voting is done in secret, but you can get some idea of how the wealthy vote by looking at the voting records in wealthy geographic areas. I refute the notion that the rich are all conservatives, and I will explain why, using Wyoming's Teton County as my example.

Teton County's largest city is Jackson. Teton County is located in northwestern Wyoming, as are Yellowstone and Grand Teton National Parks. Only a small quantity of land is privately owned in Teton County, while some level or branch of the government controls most of the property. Wyoming is a state with no inheritance or income taxes.

This low-tax environment, along with the natural beauty and recreational opportunities in and near Teton County, makes the area a magnet for the rich.

The rich people who have recently moved into Jackson like Jackson the way it is. The rich newcomers want Jackson to retain its rural western look and culture. This has led to political pressure to restrict building and development. With so little private land to start with, and restrictions placed on developing what little private land is left, land and housing prices have increased to such a level that the average working person can no longer afford to live in Jackson. The housing and land price increases have been truly amazing.

The funny thing about this influx of rich people has been the shift in politics within Teton County. The county has switched from being one of staunch conservative Republicans, similar to most of the state's counties, to being a county where liberals and conservatives are about equal in number. Teton County voted for President Ronald Reagan and the senior President George Bush by huge margins in 1980, 1984, and 1988, with total voter turnout of less than 6,000 voters for the major-party candidates. In 1992, the number of people voting increased by nearly 2,500 above that of the 1988 election and the voters gave Teton County to President Bill Clinton by about 3 percent. In 1996, Teton County again gave the county to Clinton by 1.5 percent, while the remainder of the state gave Bob Dole the election by just less than 13 percent of the vote. In 2000, George W. Bush beat Al Gore in Teton County by about 14 percent of the vote, while the state as a whole had Bush winning by 40 percent. Although Bush won Teton County, if you add the 7 percent of the vote that Green Party candidate Ralph Nader garnered to the liberal total, Bush's margin becomes only 7 percent. (This voting information is available at www.uselectionatlas.org.)

All of these rich people moved into the county and the county started voting for liberals. That's a very interesting change in voting patterns. My point here is that the political paradigm of the rich as conservative Republicans is a false paradigm. Many of the truly wealthy are liberal Democrats, and these people do not particularly like or represent the middle class.

Wealth is made up of two components. One component is the taxable income earned in the current tax year, and the other component is saved wealth and capital gains that are not taxable until sold. For example, the media often mentions that the founders of Ben & Jerry's Ice Cream received only a small salary from their company. Liberals like to use the ratio of the salary of a corporation's CEO to the salary of the lowest paid person in the company as a rough gauge of a company's social fairness. Because Ben & Jerry's was doing very well, the founders' personal wealth increased greatly, even though they received only token salaries. Their personal wealth was being held in stock, which is not taxable until the stock is sold. Even when the stock is sold, the stock is taxed at the lower capital gains rate, and no Social Security or Medicaid taxes are owed. Whatever salary the owners were receiving would pale in comparison to their increase in wealth owing to the increase in the company's stock price.

Continuing this discussion on the difference between wealth and income, let's say you are doing very well and have taxable income of $500,000 this year, but this is your first year of earning anything near this level of income, and you have very little savings. Compare this to someone who has $10 million in investments and has current earnings, not counting investment income, of $50,000. Who is richer? I would take the $10 million in the bank with the $50,000 income over the $500,000 income and no savings. When making this comparison, please consider that the $500,000 in income will be greatly reduced by income taxes, and the $10 million will grow, oftentimes tax free. Another way to compare the two situations would be to look at the effect of job loss. The $500,000 wage earner could be in immediate financial trouble upon job loss, whereas the person with $10 million in the bank would hardly be affected.

Politicians justify tax increases by attacking the rich, but their tax increase proposals are aimed at the high-income earner who may or may not be rich. If the politicians want to tax the rich, then they should tax the rich. A person who has high income for a short time may not be rich at all, but that person will be taxed as if he or she were rich. The truly rich may escape taxes all together if they have little taxable income.

If you really want to find out who the wealthy are, propose a tax on wealth and listen to who starts screaming. The truly wealthy have succeeded in lobbying for tax laws that offer all kinds of ways to protect accumulated wealth. This wealth is handed down from generation to generation in low-tax trusts. As a result, very wealthy politicians, such as the Kennedy family, don't mind taxing high wage earners because these politicians' wealth is not current income but accumulated wealth. The wealthy politicians can be charitable with your money and leave their money untouched in a trust fund. The liberal politicians then have the audacity to try to shame you into paying more taxes to an entity that is nine times larger than OPEC.

This political paradigm of the rich being free-market conservatives is not logical for other reasons. In order to accumulate great wealth, you must offer a product or service that has high profit margins. In a competitive marketplace, which we conservatives favor, high profit margins are rare. One way to get high margins is to restrict competition in the marketplace by government intervention. However, government intervention in the marketplace is not compatible with the conservatives' free-market values.

Another way to gain wealth is through the use of the courts. There is a good reason why trial lawyers actively support liberal politicians. Hoovers on Line (http://hoovers.com and do a search on "Ciresi") states that the law firm of Robins, Kaplan, Miller & Ciresi walked away with a $550 million fee when the state of Minnesota sued cigarette companies to recover the state's medical costs associated with smoking. To put this fee into some kind of perspective, $550 million is about $100 for every person in Minnesota. After receiving the large legal fees, these lawyers could now afford to move to Jackson.

The discussion of tax policy illustrates the lack of representation of the middle class and the working poor on the part of the politicians and the media. Business publications talk about tax rates and the amount of income taxes that are paid by the wealthy. These publications conveniently omit the huge burden of Social Security taxes in their argument on lower tax rates. The liberal media, which likes to represent the poor in the debate, often argues that the rich should pay more taxes. However, the term "rich" is rarely defined. The rich make a convenient, if vague, target. As I've mentioned before, the top 5 percent of taxpayers already shoulder 50 percent of the income tax burden. How much more can we drain off without creating serious disincentives to work? Higher taxes also reduce funds available for investment and philanthropy—activities that provide greater benefits to society than many, if not most, government services.

The government is such a huge entity that its need for money is also huge. There are not enough rich people to support this huge entity. For the first time in the late 1990s there were one million millionaires in the United States. If each of these millionaires paid $1 million to the government, it would pay for about half of the annual federal budget. The poor have little wealth to tax. This leaves the middle class to shoulder much of the tax burden.

The middle-income wage earner and the working poor are placed in an unenviable position. These low- and middle-income earners cannot save a great deal of money because taxes take a large portion of the wealth they produce. The lower and middle classes are in no position to take the financial risks that might lead to greater earnings. These people should have a way of reaching prosperity. Their taxes should be low or nonexistent. Taxes on their savings should not exist.

The incomes of people who do not escape the burden of Social Security taxes ($84,900 or less in 2002), but who are in the 15 percent federal tax bracket are heavily burdened by taxes. This level includes most incomes. Second incomes that do not escape the tax burden of Social Security are very heavily taxed. Second incomes are taxed at a minimum of the first income's highest tax rate. This tax burden is shared by the employer or is increased even further for the self-employed.

The Social Security tax isn't deductible from income taxes. To be taxed on money already taken by another tax is an injustice. To have income tax levied on money sent directly from your employer to the government is unconscionable. To clarify this point, if you make $50,000, the $3,825 that is your portion of the Social Security and Medicare taxes is taxed at the top federal bracket that you happen to be in.

There is nothing quite like getting taxed on a tax. And do you hear anyone sticking up for you? I don't. The liberal media are silent. Just pay the taxes and be quiet. The burden, if you are in the 27.5 percent tax bracket, is 0.275 times $3,825, which is $1,051.87. To the stock option crowd, $1,051 is nothing. To the rich who pass their wealth from gene-ration to generation using trusts, $1,051 is nothing. To most people, $1,051 is a fairly large sum of money. And these numbers do not even address the employer's portion of the Social Security and Medicare taxes, which are, after all, taxes on your income paid through your employer.

I wrote a letter to the editors of The Wall Street Journal in late 1999 to illustrate just what the tax laws meant to me. The letter was never printed. I am including an excerpt of the letter because it highlights how high taxes can be on second incomes.

> . . .With the tax system the way it is, to fully explain how much I pay in taxes gets quite complicated, so for simplicity I offer the following. My wife's salary puts every dollar I earn in a fairly high tax bracket, but my income is such that every dollar I make is still taxed for Social Security. The math works out something like this. I make about $68,000. I pay 8 percent ($5,440) to the state of Minnesota. I pay 36 percent ($24,480) to the United States in income taxes. I pay 7.65 percent ($5,202) in Social Security and Medicare taxes, and my employer matches the Social Security and Medicare tax with another $5,202 of taxes.

> I end up getting about $32,878 from my employment, and the state and federal government gets a total of $40,324 from my employment.

> Since the government gets $7,446 more out of my employment than I do, I'm assuming that the government would want to know of any change in my work status. I'm seriously contemplating quitting the workforce. I like my job, but I also value my time. I think I add a great deal of wealth to our economy, but I can't shake this feeling that I'm being abused by the government getting $7,446 more than I do from my employment. . . .

# CHAPTER SIX

# SOCIAL SECURITY

After the Great Depression, there were no doubt a number of elderly people who did not have sufficient retirement funds. The government wanted to help these people, but probably did not want the program to appear to be a politically unpopular welfare system. The program that the government came up with was the Social Security system. The Social Security system was sold to the electorate as a retirement and insurance fund, and the majority of people still view Social Security as a retirement and insurance fund.

Is Social Security a retirement fund? In the liberal paradigm it is. You pay into the system, and the government uses some of that money to help present-day retirees, and saves some of the money so that you will have it when you retire. You pay now and others will pay for you in the future. In the liberal paradigm, you are paying only 6.2 percent of your wages into the Social Security system. The return received for the 6.2 percent Social Security tax is viewed as a sound investment.

In the conservative paradigm, Social Security is minimally a retirement fund and mostly an income redistribution fund. Retirement funds are normally invested in hard assets such as real estate, stocks, and bonds, with the expectation that the hard assets will yield earnings and increase in value with time. The money that you pay into a retirement fund starts producing additional growth for your fund. The fund grows with this combination of your additions and the earnings that the fund generates. After many years, earnings from the fund start to surpass annual additions to the fund. Eventually the size of the fund will enable the retirees to live off of the fund's earnings, and if these earnings are not adequate, then additional funds may be drawn from the fund balance over the person's anticipated life span.

For more than twenty years, I worked for a company that had a great profit sharing plan. The annual company contribution to this plan averaged almost 15 percent of wages and the plan had paid out a minimum of 15 percent of base wages for many years prior to my employment. In the first years of my employment, I looked forward to the company contribution to my fund. The people who had worked there longer were not as interested in the annual contribution as they were in the earnings of their fund. At about ten years of employment, the earnings on the fund started to exceed the annual company contribution. For people who had been employed for twenty years or more, the annual company contribution was insignificant compared to the earnings of the fund. What does this little story have to do with Social Security?

Because most of the current Social Security tax revenues are paid out to current retirees, this return on investments is lost. Social Security payments depend almost totally on tax collections from people who are currently working and from their employers. Paying for others' retirement out of current taxes becomes a problem as the retired population grows at a greater rate than the working population. In other words, the Social Security system as a retirement program is not actuarially sound.

The majority of the money you and your employer pay into the Social Security system is not available to be invested. Most of the money is paid out to present retirees. Any tax money collected beyond what is presently required for current Social Security expenditures is used to buy government bonds. Because most of the money is paid out to present retirees, you will receive little earnings on most of the money you put into the Social Security system.

The conservative paradigm acknowledges that you are paying 12.4 percent of your wages into Social Security. This is twice as much as the obvious 6.2 percent tax rate because your employer's 6.2 percent payroll tax is seen as a tax on your employment. The return you receive in retirement benefits from Social Security is terrible when you consider that you paid in 12.4 percent of your salary annually over your career.

Another reason Social Security is viewed as an income redistribution fund by conservatives is that there is no fund balance to be distributed to your heirs. When you die, then the number of people drawing funds from the Social Security program has been reduced by one.

If you are going to be drawing Social Security funds out of the system in the future, I would be very concerned about funding the program out of present workers' wages, their employers' matching payroll taxes, and the few government bonds held by the Social Security administration. I was born in 1956 and am part of the bulge of the population increase that took place after World War II and the Korean War. There is a common misconception about what is called the baby boom generation. This common misconception is that a large number of children were born in the late 1940s. In actuality the greatest number of births in our country occurred in the mid- to late 1950s, with 1957 being the year with the greatest number of births. When the people from our age group start to retire, there will be a huge demand for Social Security retirement funds. My concern is that the working population will not tolerate the taxation required to meet our retirement needs. If I had to, I would predict that resources for this group of retirees will be rationed if Social Security is allowed to maintain its present course.

What about the surplus Social Security tax that is collected now? I previously stated that this money is currently being used to purchase government bonds. The surplus Social Security tax money is then spent on current government needs just as any other tax money is spent. The surplus Social Security tax money becomes in effect just a nondeductible income tax on incomes of less than $84,900. When the bonds come due, the federal government will have to buy them back with additional tax money. I don't think the taxpayers from the generation that will have to fund our retirement will put up with paying additional money to redeem the bonds to further fund our retirement needs.

If I wanted to create a program that highlighted all the things I don't like about unnecessary government, I would have created the Social Security system. The list of things I don't like includes:

1) The working poor are subject to the tax. The poor pay money out of their meager earnings to people who are in many cases better off than themselves.

2) The tax is an unjust tax (see chapter 8) whereby money is forcibly taken from one person and given to another.

3) The Social Security tax is in no way deductible within the income tax system. You pay income tax on Social Security tax money.

4) For those currently in the workforce, the rate of return on the money paid into the Social Security system will be terrible.

5) Half of the Social Security tax is hidden and paid by the employer.

6) The fact that employees are not made aware that the employer is taking some of the employee's wages to pay the Social Security and Medicare tax contributes to bad employee/employer relationships.

7) The taxes collected in excess of what is required to currently fund the Social Security program are being used to pay for other government activity without the need to pass additional tax increase legislation.

Suppose you were approached by your bank and asked to deposit 12.4 percent of your pretax earnings into an account every couple of weeks. This money would be withdrawn from your account and transferred to the account of another bank customer who had been a customer longer than you. After 45 years of paying 12.4 percent of your earnings to the bank, you would get your money back in small, monthly payments with little or no earnings. This payback would come from new customers of the bank, since the money you deposited has already been given to other bank customers. When you die, the account will be closed by the bank, and your heirs will not receive any future payments. Would you sign up for this? I would personally laugh at a person trying to sell such an absurd program to me. Is there any wonder why the government has to use force to get you to join an identical program called Social Security?

The federal government should get out of the retirement business. The problem with the government getting out of the retirement business is that the government now has a huge financial obligation to the people who have been paying into the system. How will the government honor this huge financial obligation?

I said previously that hard assets, such as real estate and financial instruments, back retirement funds in the private market. The federal government is a huge holder of real estate—a landowner so large as to own almost one-third of the land within the United States. I propose that the government sell some of its land to fund its Social Security obligations. This extra land on the market would serve a dual purpose, as it would also have the secondary effect of lowering land values, which would increase the availability and affordability of housing. I also propose removing taxes on savings for most people. Let people finance their own retirement without the government taking a high percentage of the earnings on savings in taxes, resulting in the creation of additional incentive for people to save for their retirement.

# CHAPTER SEVEN

# GOVERNMENT GROWTH

How did our government get so big? There are a number of reasons, including the government's budgeting methods and the inadequate information provided to taxpayers.

Milton Friedman, the Nobel prize-winning economist, has written extensively on the history of our economy. I summarized Friedman's work in the first part of this chapter, but to review the entire updated work, which I highly recommend, please see Friedman's *Free to Choose*, which should be available both in book and video form at your local library or bookstore.

Until the Great Depression of the late 1920s and 1930s, the United States economy was basically free. The Great Depression was the beginning of the end of our unregulated, low-tax environment. It's common knowledge that the Great Depression was caused by the failure of markets. Overspeculation led to an overpriced stock market that finally collapsed. The collapse of the stock market brought down the economy as well. This "common knowledge" is severely wrong, and the misinterpretation has cost us enormously.

The United States, prior to the Great Depression, had made huge economic strides. The one problem that kept resurfacing during those times was the boom-and-bust cycles caused by a lack of adequate control over the amount of money in the system. Even with the boom-and-bust cycles, however, real incomes made enormous strides.

Many people try to justify these growth rates due to huge advancements in technology, but let's be truthful. I know of no time in history when we were making the kinds of advances that we are making today. As one of my teacher friends says, innovation is the new combination of known facts. With the huge expansion of known facts, the new possible combinations become seemingly infinite.

Today a single farmer has the ability to feed hundreds of people. Our automobiles are truly works of wonder that speed us to our intended destinations while emitting minute amounts of pollution. Airplanes can fly us anywhere in the world in hours. People live healthy lives well into their eighties and nineties. Spaceships zip in and out of our atmosphere many times a year. It's astounding. You would think our salaries would be increasing at an enormous rate. Why aren't they? My answer to this question is that the government is a huge consumer of wealth. The government takes vast sums of money from us and wastes it or gives it to others. Without this waste and funds transfer, we would all have a much higher standard of living.

How did government reach this size? In the conservative paradigm, our monetary system failed and caused the Great Depression. I do not know if there was too little knowledge of money or if the system was not adequate to do anything about it, but the money supply shrank enormously. The supply of money was not adequate for the size of the economy. To borrow a line from the musical *Hello Dolly*, "Money is like manure: spread it around and it makes things grow, pile it up and it makes a big stink." I would add, "Apply too little manure or fertilizer and little grows." Applying too little money caused the Great Depression. If you read this and disagree, please tell me how a stock market crash and overspeculation can cause a depression. We had an example of the stock market crashing in 1987, but the Federal Reserve made money available to the markets and the economy did not miss a beat. I can't stress enough: the Great Depression was caused not by a failure of the marketplace, but by the failure of the government to adequately supply money to the marketplace.

According to conventional wisdom, however, the free market was responsible for the failure of the economy. Therefore, because people had the cause wrong, their solutions to the problem were not likely to be very helpful. They were, in fact, very unhelpful. The government passed trade restrictions and the depression deepened. The government gave labor greater power and the depression deepened. The government created work programs and the depression deepened. Finally, the government created more money to finance World War II and the depression ended.

Common knowledge, and now political power as well, came to support the idea that the government had to be intimately involved in the economy. An even more outlandish lesson drawn from the end of the depression is the absurd assertion—which I still occasionally hear—that wars are somehow good for the economy. The political paradigm had indeed shifted. Too bad for us! Too bad government also became involved with the social aspects of life.

Many people believe that what they are currently thinking is new and original, but I believe there is very little new thought. Most of what we are talking and writing about has been written and talked about for centuries. Greek philosophers debated the role of government thousands of years ago. The pilgrims created and signed the Mayflower Compact prior to the formation of our own government. When Thomas Jefferson and company wrote the United States Constitution, they were not starting from scratch with a new set of ideas, but implementing political thought that had been in circulation for a long time.

History has thousands of examples of government being oppressive to its people. Oppression is the reason why most people came to the United States in the first place. The early arrivals to the shores of North America were attempting to escape not only religious persecution but other forms of government oppression as well. When our founders wrote the Constitution, they had a great deal of history behind them and that history told them that limited government was the best form of government. Our founding fathers thought government's role was to establish rules of trade and to defend the country. That's a pretty short list.

Milton Friedman adds to this list the protection of innocent third parties, but I think it's clear that the conservative paradigm holds that smaller government is better government.

In the liberal paradigm, government is required to put limits on society and the marketplace. Government can never get too big. There is always some wrong to be righted, some injustice to be made just. The liberal views the government as being by Solomon-like figures blessed with great knowledge and fairness.

The conservative paradigm recognizes constitutionally mandated government functions as necessary government. There is, however, much government action that has greatly exceeded the bounds of the Constitution, and this we consider to be unnecessary government. To highlight how a conservative views this unnecessary government, I offer the following example.

A sea lamprey is a parasitic animal that attaches itself to a fish, from which the sea lamprey obtains its nourishment. A lamprey is a truly ugly animal. Lampreys invaded the Upper Great Lakes when the Welland Canal was built around Niagara Falls, and they had a devastating affect on the fish populations in the Upper Great Lakes. When the lamprey is small, it has little or no effect on the fish, but as the lamprey grows and takes a higher percentage of the fish's total nutrition intake, the fish begins to feel the burden. The fish may survive the lamprey's attachment for a time, but it will not prosper. It is just too difficult a task for the fish to eat enough to satisfy both animals' needs. Conservatives view the effect of unnecessary government on its people in the same way they view a sea lamprey's effect on a fish. It's difficult to meet your own personal needs, society's charitable needs, and the government's needs—especially as the government's needs continue to grow. If the government take is small, you hardly notice. If the government take is large, you do not prosper.

Free-market systems have produced great wealth, and our government has grown tremendously by siphoning off some of this wealth from the economy. In a representative republic, for the government to be able to sustain such growth, the public must be convinced that the government needs additional funds. How is the government able to convince the public that it needs additional funding? One way is to confuse the public when addressing budget matters. Government bureaucracies have an interesting way of discussing budgets. I refer to this way of looking at budgeting as the bureaucratic budgeting paradigm.

Government bureaucracies compare budget changes relative to the current proposed budget, not the previous year's budget. In the nongovernment paradigm, budgets are compared to the previous year's budget.

In the bureaucratic budgeting paradigm, the budgeting process works like this. Let's say Government Department A had a budget of $1,000 in fiscal year 2002 and projected a 10 percent increase for fiscal year 2003, raising the amount to $1,100. The 10 percent proposed budget increase is submitted and reviewed, and the budget reviewers say that a 10 percent increase is too great. Department A will have to make do with a 5 percent increase in fiscal year 2003, which leaves a budget of $1,050. The government bureaucracy will talk of this budget change as being a 5 percent budget cut. They were supposed to get $1,100 in fiscal year 2003, but Department A will only get $1,050 in fiscal year 2003, a 5 percent reduction.

In the nongovernment paradigm, the budget went from $1,000 in fiscal year 2002 to $1,050 in fiscal year 2003, which is a 5 percent increase. In the nongovernment paradigm, the budget was slated to be 10 percent greater than the previous period, but now the budget will only be 5 percent greater. In the nongovernment paradigm, this is a budget increase of 5 percent over the last period. When government officials talk of a budget cut, they are usually talking about a cut to a proposed budget, not an actual reduction from the previous year's budget.

Until I understood this, I was always confused by government budgeting discussions. I would see my taxes going up, and I would see the government expanding, but when I would listen to the budget discussions, the talk would always be about budgets being cut. It never made any sense.

Another comparison to highlight this difference in paradigms is an example of a salary increase. Let's say you were expecting to receive a 10 percent raise from your employer. After much consideration, your employer decides he or she can only afford to give you a 6 percent raise. You don't tell people that you received a 4 percent pay cut because you received a 6 percent raise instead of the expected 10 percent raise. You tell people you received a 6 percent raise.

When entering into discussions on government budgets, you need to pointedly ask the government official what the current budget is and what the next budget is going to be. You should also demand from your media source that the previous year's budget and the proposed budget numbers be made available to you so you can decide for yourself the implications of the change in the budget. The media is supposed to be fair and balanced. All too often, however, I find that this is not the case.

One of my pet peeves is the excessive media attention given to energy prices, but the total failure to notice many tax increases. If the price of oil increases, the media people make it the lead story on the evening news or the top headline in the daily paper. On the other hand, taxes constantly go up, costing the consumer far more than the energy price increases, and we don't hear a thing from the media.

For example, I received a memo at work in late 2000 with the title of "Important Payroll & Tax Information." Contained in this memo was the fact that the 6.2 percent Social Security tax will apply to the first $80,400 in income earned in 2001. This was up from $76,200 in 2000 and $72,600 in 1999, and will increase to $84,900 in 2002. The amount of tax you paid if you are in this income bracket went from $4724.40 in 2000 to $4,984.80 in 2001, an increase of $260.40 to you and an increase of $260.40 to your employer. Why does this never make the news, but if the price of gasoline goes up a nickel it is a huge news story? At least energy prices sometime go down. Taxes never seem to go down.

Let's say you drive 30,000 miles a year and your vehicle get 15 miles per gallon of gasoline. In this example you would use 2,000 gallons of gasoline per year. For every nickel of increase in the price of gas, your annual increase in payments for gasoline would be $100. For argument's sake, let's say you receive a salary or wage increase of $1,000 per year. If you are a wage earner in the 27.5 percent federal tax bracket, with a state tax of 4.5 percent and a 7.65 percent Social Security and Medicare tax, you will pay $396.50 in increased taxes on this $1,000 salary or wage increase. Your employer will also see a Social Security and Medicare tax increase of $76.50 because of your wage increase, but for simplicity's sake these numbers are not included in this example. Your tax increase would be equivalent to the price of gas going up roughly $0.19 per gallon at a gas usage of 2,000 gallons per year.

If you read this and think a $0.19 increase per year doesn't sound like much, consider the following. The retail gasoline price, including taxes, was about $0.299 back in 1970. If the price of gasoline had increased at the rate discussed above for thirty years, the price of gas would be about $6 per gallon, not counting any of the additional gas tax increases that have since been added, in 2000. The media plays up the story of higher energy prices, but never a word on higher taxes.

If you want to try something interesting, make a list of the amounts you pay for everything, including food, sales taxes, clothing, property taxes, insurance, income taxes, interest, Social Security and Medicare taxes, entertainment, gasoline, gasoline taxes, house payments or rent, and other miscellaneous taxes, such as taxes on the purchase of hunting and fishing gear, automobiles, tires, and airline tickets. For the majority of people, taxes will be the largest expenditure by far. The government didn't get nine times bigger than OPEC without taking a lot of your money.

Another reason the government is so big is that citizens do not have free choice in the purchase of the government's services. If you don't buy the government's products or services through the payment of your taxes, you go to jail, pay a fine, or have your life ruined in any number of ways. Is it fair for the government to take your money through taxation, to be redistributed to others?

# CHAPTER EIGHT

# THE FAIRNESS OF TAXATION FOR TRANSFER PAYMENTS

L iberals take the moral high ground when discussing tax policy. In the liberal paradigm, tax choice comes down to either reducing taxes (which saves money for the wealthy, who don't really need it) or turning the money over to the government to be distributed to the less fortunate and to operate vital government agencies. Liberals believe they are playing the part of Robin Hood by taking from the rich and giving to the poor. In actuality, the tax collector is the Sheriff of Nottingham, taking from the people and allowing most of the money to be swallowed by the government bureaucracies and transferred to the non-poor.

The liberal will describe the taxation of the wealthy to transfer the money to the poor as an act of justice or fairness. The conservative views this transfer not as a transfer between the rich and the poor, but as a transfer between the wealth-producing economy and the wealth-consuming government bureaucracy and the groups that benefit from these government takings.

The conservative argument against taxation is that taxpayers have earned the money so they should be able to keep more of it. Although the conservative argument sounds greedy, it is not based on greed but on the knowledge that the government will waste a great portion of the taxes collected and redistribute much of the wealth to the non-poor. Conservatives should argue their position on taxation by taking the high moral ground: the taking of wealth from the nongovernment to supply the government leads to an overall lower standard of living for ourselves and our fellow countrymen.

When you are forced to give your money to the government, a large portion is wasted or transferred to non-poor people. I do not know how much money is spent on social programs or how much is intended to be transferred from one person to another by the federal government, but it is a large amount. For argument's sake, let's say the amount is $1 trillion, which is about half of the federal budget. This $1 trillion is admittedly a very rough approximation, but the gist of the argument will not change over a few hundred billion dollars. From the numbers included in the appendix, you can see that Social Security is budgeted at $433.1 billion, income security at $269.8 billion and Medicare at $217.5 billion. Just these three programs add up to $920.4 billion. This $920 billion does not include the $172 billion that Health and Human Services has budgeted. There are also transfer payments imbedded in the other budget items, such as agriculture, but it is really not my intent to dig that deeply into the budget details.

Let's assume that one out of ten of us is poor. One out of ten would leave us with at most 30 million poor people. $1 trillion divided by 30 million people is $33,333 per person. A poor family of four should be getting $133,332 if all the money taxed were actually given to the poor. Ask some person who relies on the government for assistance if he or she is getting this much money. If there were 50 million poor people in the United States, the numbers would be $20,000 per person and $80,000 for a family of four. I don't believe that one in six of us is poor. Where does the money go? My guess is that most of the money ends up paying for salaries and other expenses inherent in large bureaucracies and being transferred to the non-poor.

One of the things that I found very interesting in Milton Friedman's work *Free to Choose* was his discussion of the accumulation of wealth in

Washington, D.C. I went to the government's census Web site (www. census.gov) to verify the information. One would think that most of the wealth in the United States would be concentrated in the financial and industrial centers such as New York, Los Angeles, San Francisco, Chicago, Dallas, St. Louis, Denver, Miami, Seattle, and so on. In actuality, the counties with the second and seventh-highest household incomes in the United States in 2000 were suburbs of Washington, D.C., the seat of government. I think it terribly wrong to take money that was presented to the people as being earmarked for the poor, and instead pay it to government bureaucracies and the non-poor in the name of helping the poor.

In the conservative paradigm, wealth is a reward for meeting someone's need for a product or service. When this wealth is forcibly taken and transferred to someone not producing a needed product or service, it hurts both parties. When free exchange is changed to forced exchange, the lesson learned from the pursuit of meeting someone's needs is lost. The need to fit into the exchange system is lost, and the self-worth of the person on the receiving end of the forced exchange is reduced. The recipient becomes dependent instead of independent, and may start to believe that he or she deserves to benefit from the forced exchange. The forced exchange may encourage unhealthy personal decisions. A December 9, 1993, *New York Post* column by Ben Wattenburg discusses the issue of unmarried welfare mothers having additional children at least partially for the purpose of receiving a larger welfare check. If women are bearing children for this reason, then I feel great sorrow for the children.

If redistribution funds are to exist, then they should go to the poor. Obviously, from the above example, the poor are not the primary recipients of the funds. In one of the previous chapters I wrote about Social Security and how it is a redistribution fund. It is a message that I'm afraid many of you will not want to hear. The Social Security taxes that you have paid are no different from any other tax you have paid in that the money went to the government and it has been spent or redistributed. If you collect Social Security income, you are taking the funds from a current taxpayer. If you collect income security funds you are taking funds from a current taxpayer. If you take any kind of payment from the government, or if you are attending an educational establishment that is funded by the government, then you are taking money from a current taxpayer.

Many people never view themselves as accepting funds from the government, or as becoming dependent or partially dependent on the government, but it is an extremely easy and common thing to do. I am a prime example. My son has a disorder known as Fragile X. I discuss this in greater detail in the chapter on abortion, but suffice it to say that he is mentally disabled. Our family has relied on the public schools since my son was in the fourth grade. This was not so much an economic choice for us, but simply a consequence of the fact that no one else offered services for the disabled that were anywhere near what our public school system offered. We have not involved ourselves with other government programs. Now, however, we have faced and continue to face a number of dilemmas as our son reaches adulthood.

The first dilemma was the Selective Service. We received a letter asking that our son fill out the Selective Service registration card. I explained the situation on the card and returned it. A new letter appeared, stating that my son had to sign the card or face potential legal action. I explained the situation again, but had my son sign the card with his inch-high signature in an area that was about a quarter of an inch high. The fact that our son was going to face legal action from the Selective Service was enough to prompt my wife to sign up with the Social Security agency. If our son is designated as disabled by the Social Security Administration, then Selective Service will recognize the disability, and he will not be drafted. We are not poor, but our son now gets the minimum amount available in a monthly Social Security check.

How do we justify collecting Social Security? A number of ways. One, we are keeping our son from possibly being drafted. Two, we pay enormous amounts of money in taxes. The small amount our son receives somehow balances what we pay. Three, if we die, then our son is in the Medicaid system and his expenses will be covered. We have asked relatives to look after our son, and I believe they would do it, but this gives our son one more option in the event of our untimely deaths.

We are trying to prepare for the future care of our son, but we are not yet in that financial position. In the meantime, we have chosen to enter our son into the government transfer payment system. But is this action fair?

Is it fair for the government to forcibly take money from one person and give it to another? Noted economist Walter Williams makes the argument that it is clearly not right for the government to forcibly take money from one to give to another. Williams' argument follows.

If I were walking down the street and a person with less wealth than me decided to forcibly take my wealth, then society would charge this individual with perpetrating a crime against me. To carry the example further, let's say that instead of acting as an individual, the person with less wealth than me joins together with two friends and the three of them democratically vote two to one in favor of taking my wealth. The three confront me and force me to give them my money. Is this robbery? It was, after all, a democratic decision. Now let us further argue that this person gathers together a group of ten people. The ten democratically vote six to four to take my money and to give the money to the three poorest people of their group. The ten confront me and I am forced to turn my money over to them, and they in turn give the money to the three poorest of their group. Is this robbery? It was democratically decided to take my money. The group was planning to give the money to the poorest members of the group, so the group had good intentions.

Now change the number of people in the example to a hundred people, or a thousand people, or a congressional district, or a state or national legislature. Is not the forcible taking of my wealth to give to others still robbery? If you do not consider it robbery, how big of a group do you need to have it change from robbery to something other than robbery? Did the fact that people democratically voted, or the number of people who concurred, or the fact that in their view it was a just cause, make the act of forcibly taking my money any less unjust? I think not. Yet this ability to take from some to give to others is the law of our land, and in my view it's the foundation from which our huge government has grown to be nine times larger than OPEC.

We are searching for non-government solutions for our son's future, but it's a struggle. Everything revolves around the government programs. We will continue the search. Our family situation highlights the problem of taking from the government. My immediate family has fairly high income, yet even we are receiving government payments. How might we reduce dependence on the government? My suggestion is to create a strong private charitable organization (which will be discussed in chapter twenty-one), and to modify the Constitution.

# CHAPTER NINE

# PROPOSAL TO REDUCE TAXATION AND THE SIZE OF THE GOVERNMENT

The Sixteenth Amendment to the United States Constitution gave the federal government an unlimited ability to tax incomes, both individual and business. Here is the text:

Article XVI – *The congress shall have power to lay and collect taxes on incomes, from whatever source derived, without apportionment among the several States, and without regard to any census or enumeration.*

The government has grown to be a colossal entity with this taxing authority. I believe that adopting the Sixteenth Amendment without placing limits on how much tax could be levied was a major mistake. To try to reduce the government's size one program at a time will be a significant task, and will bring huge political forces out to combat cuts in each program. The one way to stop the government's growth would be to limit government taxing and borrowing authority. To do this in an amendment to the Constitution would lead to one large political battle instead of a thousand individual battles.

I previously stated the following:

- All business taxes are really hidden sales taxes, so businesses do not really pay taxes but act as tax collection agencies for hidden taxes.

- Wealth consists of current income and saved wealth.

- Incomes that see high federal tax rates while still paying Social Security taxes have the highest marginal tax rates and cause the economy to discourage the creation and retention of jobs in this salary range.

- The working poor should not have to pay taxes.

With the above in mind, I would like to replace the Sixteenth Amendment with the following:

> Revised Article XVI – *The congress shall have the power to lay and collect taxes on individuals' incomes, from whatever source derived, at both a marginal and aggregate rate not to exceed 25 percent. This power to tax incomes will not apply to any income below a level that is determined to be that income which encompasses all of the income of the lowest 25 percent of income earners. The congress shall have the power to tax individuals' wealth, if that wealth is greater than $5,000,000 in constant 2001 dollars, at a rate not to exceed 0.5 percent of the value of the wealth, regardless of how the wealth is held.*
>
> *The United States government may not borrow an amount of money exceeding 10 percent of the income and wealth taxes previously mentioned in any given year, unless there is a declared war.*

You may ask how the wealth figure of $5,000,000 and the tax rate of 0.5 percent were derived. I consider anyone with that much wealth to be independently wealthy, and I think everyone should have an opportunity to reach this level of wealth before the government would be able to collect its wealth tax. As for the 0.5 percent wealth tax, I've read that historically there is about a 1 percent real rate of return on investments. The 0.5 percent tax would result in there being a 50 percent tax on these earnings.

In the conservative paradigm, the people's financial well-being should be constitutionally protected. Limiting taxation of income would be a great change to the Constitution and would help achieve this objective.

# CHAPTER TEN

# THE CONSTITUTION

Everything I read or heard about democracies when I was growing up was positive. Educators told us that we were very lucky to be born in a country with a democratically elected government. This always puzzled me.

I was raised in Minnesota, which was and is one of the more liberal states in our great nation. I can't remember anyone for whom my parents voted ever winning a statewide election. Our family would sit around the kitchen table after dinner talking about some political person whose ideas my parents held in contempt. This person would later win the election. The people who were elected were very liberal (Hubert Humphrey, Walter Mondale, Don Frazier) and they did not represent my parents' beliefs at all. It also seemed to me at the time that most elected leaders, both nationally and internationally, left a lot to be desired.

As I learned more, I found out that even Hitler's government had initially been elected democratically. Was democracy the best system? How could it be? I came to the conclusion that democracy was not the greatest idea. I also saw that countries under communism, socialism, fascism, or monarchy were a lot worse off than we were, so those types of systems were obviously not the answer. I came to the conclusion that what we needed was a friendly dictator. The only problem was that I didn't know where to find a friendly dictator. I also didn't know how the friendly dictator would come to power, or how the friendly dictator would be replaced by another friendly dictator when the first friendly dictator died. At the time, I thought this to be an unsolvable problem and I forgot about the whole thing.

At some point in my life, it finally dawned on me that this friendly dictator that I had been looking for when I was quite young was our Constitution.

Our country's founders realized that a pure democracy was not the optimal form of government, so they formed a constitutional republic in which the individual was assumed to be granted rights not from the government but from God. Individual rights were not the government's to grant or take away. The governing power did not reside entirely with the majority, but was limited by the rights of each individual. The founders understood the natural tendency of governments of any type, including democracies, to usurp power from the people, so government power was restricted.

My basic criticism of democracies is that there are simply too many losers. Many elections are won by very small margins. This means that the will of a large percentage of the people is not being represented by the person who was elected. In a perfect world, everyone would see his or her interests represented. In a democracy of any type, fulfilling everyone's wishes just isn't possible. Thus, as many decisions as possible should be left not to elected officials but to individuals and the marketplace.

An example of a political decision that would not meet everyone's wishes would be a local school board decision on whether to have sex education as part of the curriculum. The board must decide whether the school will have sex education. The parents on either side of the issue believe they are right in their position on the subject, but regardless which decision the school board makes, one group will not be satisfied. One group will lose. Compare this to a free-market decision, such as what you will have for lunch. You may want Asian food, you may want fast food, you may want a particular form of fast food, you may want a lot to eat, or you may want little to eat. In a free market you get what you want—exactly what you want. If someone else decides he or she wants something different for lunch, he or she is free to choose that alternative. There are no losers; there are just satisfied consumers. Isn't this personal satisfaction what we should strive for with the political system?

The 2000 presidential election also calls into question the legitimacy of the whole voting process. With a strong and enforced constitution, the election process becomes much less important.

In the conservative paradigm, the Constitution is viewed as the governing law. In the liberal paradigm, the Constitution is interpreted much more loosely. The conservative paradigm argues that the Constitution should be broadened to limit taxing authority. In the liberal paradigm, the Constitution is interpreted to broaden the role of government. Those of us within the conservative paradigm wish to be—at a minimum—ruled by laws, but our ultimate wish is to be self-ruled by a shared moral code of conduct.

# CHAPTER ELEVEN

# THE RULE OF LAW AND RULE BY INDIVIDUAL MORALS

First, a discussion of constitutional law. The conservative paradigm argues that the framers of the Constitution intended the federal government to have little governing power. The Constitution granted the federal government very limited authority. The majority of the governing power was to reside with the states. The thought was that if the people did not like what their state was doing politically, the residents could always vote with their feet and relocate to a different state that more closely reflected their wishes. The states would end up in competition, and this competition would lead the states to try to optimize the function and quality of the state. The reason the Constitution was designed in this manner was because the greatest fear of our founders was that the federal government would eventually become oppressive—as had all previously existing governments.

When you apply this state competition idea to some modern-day programs, you can see the beauty of the idea. Say some states had Social Security and some states didn't. If you really didn't like the

Social Security program and resided in a state that had Social Security, you could move to a state that didn't participate in the program.

Although limited federal government was the wish of the writers of the Constitution, efforts to limit federal power have obviously failed. The start of this failure can be traced to the Civil War. It gained momentum during the Great Depression, when the majority of policymakers in both the United States and abroad had come to believe that capitalism had failed and government needed to be involved in the marketplace. It may have culminated with our elected Senate and House, completely disregarding the Constitution and passing a campaign finance law that the lawmakers knew violated the First Amendment by placing restrictions on political speech. Many of our constitutional amendments are routinely ignored, but the violators suffer no repercussions. I would like to see a constitution that restricted government and that would not be able to be ignored. I make no recommendations on how this could become a reality.

I believe policymakers worldwide are rethinking the concept of government involvement in markets. The intellectual tide is turning toward free markets and away from government regulation and control. There are now governments that are trying to institute more market-friendly policies with little government intervention and low tax burdens. Perhaps, with the ability for free people to move capital and themselves, the countries will adapt the role of the states envisioned by our constitutional writers. People and capital will move to the countries that adopt policies that maximize freedom. We may have to start honoring our constitution in order to stay competitive.

The rule of law is based on the Constitution. The Constitution should be the framework of law that rules us as a people. The Constitution requires that everyone, regardless of social or political standing, obey the law. In addition, every citizen must be treated equally by the law. The Constitution demands that laws, independent of who is in political power, rule us as a people.

The liberal interpretation of the rule of law is entirely different from the conservative interpretation. In the liberal paradigm, the rule of law is about power. The "golden rule" is the maxim that one should behave towards others as one would have others behave toward oneself.

There is an old joke that defines the golden rule as "who owns the gold, rules." There is a similar maxim in the liberal paradigm of law. Whoever controls the law holds the power. In the liberal world, if you do not get the results you want legislatively or by popular vote, you try to challenge the decision by bringing the issue into the court system. Please keep in mind that this is the view from the conservative perspective. If you are liberal you may find it a bit harsh, but this is the conservative view.

Former Supreme Court Justice Byron White sums up this conservative view of judicial activism in his dissent in the *Roe v. Wade* abortion decision. Justice White, a Kennedy-appointed justice, said in part the following:

> . . . *With all due respect, I dissent. I find nothing in the language or history of the Constitution to support the court's judgment. The court simply fashions and announces a new constitutional right for pregnant mothers . . . and, with scarcely any reason or authority for its action, invests that right with sufficient substance to override most existing state abortion statutes. The upshot is that the people and the legislatures of the 50 States are constitutionally disentitled to weigh the relative importance of the continued existence and development of the fetus, on the one hand, against a spectrum of possible impacts on the mother, on the other hand. As an exercise of raw judicial power, the court perhaps has authority to do what it does today; but, in my view, its judgment is an improvident and extravagant exercise of the power of judicial review that the Constitution extends to this Court.*

There are many examples of liberal laws that, at least within the conservative paradigm, have no constitutional basis, yet are dictated by the courts or upheld by the courts. These include laws governing the environment, abortion, free speech and obscenity, gun control, the establishment of inheritance taxes, and so on. In the case of all of these, the courts have implemented laws that couldn't pass in legislatures or have upheld laws that are either not addressed in the Constitution or are in direct conflict with the Constitution.

I will expand upon this idea using the First Amendment as an example. In the conservative paradigm, the First Amendment is seen to address only political speech. We believe government has not only the right but also the duty to protect children and other unwilling people from obscene and suggestive material. In the conservative paradigm, it is also believed to be in society's best interest to promote moral behavior.

As the old saying goes, the definition of character is your behavior when you know that no one else will find out about your actions. Most people would not visit a theater showing adult entertainment because of the fear of being seen going into such a place. As these constraints have been removed by the Internet, movie rentals, and cable television, which offer the ability to bring pornographic material into the privacy of your home or hotel room without the public at large being aware of your actions, the porn industry has expanded. Those who financially support these industries by buying these products hurt our youth, or at least the youth who are trying to be moral, by ultimately lowering the moral standards of our society. The buyers of these materials are participating in an immoral act by giving financial incentives to the entertainers to do their immoral acts, and by allowing, even if unintentionally, the viewing of this material by the young.

The shame that should be associated with partaking in this adult entertainment industry does not keep large corporations and their stockholders from profiting from the role once delegated to the sleazy adult entertainment entrepreneur. Major hotel, entertainment and communications companies willingly and actively partake in this immoral industry.

Conservative politicians will occasionally try to establish, by law, certain public standards for things such as television, the Internet, and adult entertainment. Liberals attack these efforts as an affront to free speech and a violation of the First Amendment.

I am easily confused, and censorship is another of the things that confuses me. Do we not already have censorship? It seems to me that regular broadcast TV is not allowed to show adult-rated features. And why can't the TV stations show these features? Isn't it because the government has passed laws that—as part of a television station's broadcast licensing agreement—prevent the airing of this kind of material? Is this not government censorship? There are also laws limiting what people may display in public places, such as on billboards. My point is that we already have censorship, and I believe this is a good thing.

I believe the First Amendment has been used to force minority values on the majority. An example of this is the sale of most, if not all, adult material and adult entertainment. I'm sure the voting majorities within most cities or towns would not want this material and entertainment available in their cities or towns. The majority ends up having to tolerate these things because court rulings determine that pornography has the right to exist under the First Amendment. I don't understand how the courts reason that businesses that make money on immorality have any rights protected by the First Amendment.

When liberals bring up the First Amendment, conservatives run to the exits. We need to argue the fact that there is already censorship, and that having some censorship is a great thing to protect children and other unwilling people from immoral fare. The political debate should be on how much censorship we should have.

What is needed in our country—and it's a large part of what made our country great—is not the rule of law, but rule by individual morals. In the conservative paradigm, people who rule themselves with a high moral code are held in the highest esteem. From a standpoint of total cost, being self-ruled by individual morals has the lowest total cost.

Our morals are our personal law. If our moral standards are higher than the legal standards of the law, then there is no need for enforcement. Compliance with the law is 100 percent and the cost of the law enforcement is zero. This is how my neighborhood is. I do not worry about having anything stolen by my neighbors. The people who live in my neighborhood have moral standards higher than the law. There is little or no law enforcement cost. The total cost of law enforcement is low.

If our moral standards are lower than the legal standards, then law enforcement keeps us from breaking the law. Compliance with the law will be less than 100 percent, however, because enforcement will not always take place. There will be costs involved in replacing what is stolen, in trying to avoid having things stolen, and in law enforcement.

Even though they have little wealth to protect, people who live in the poorer inner cities of our country spend much of their limited wealth on crime avoidance, owing to the frequency with which laws are broken in these areas. The total cost of crime is quite high for these people and includes costs such as lack of employment opportunities because of the fact that businesses that can afford to locate in lawful areas will avoid unlawful areas.

Our laws are a set of rules that are supposed to be followed. Almost everyone tries to stay within the law, either out of moral conviction or out of fear of enforcement. Lawyers are sometimes employed to figure out what can be done without actually breaking the law. People will sometime be within the letter of the law, but not necessarily in the spirit of the law. Everyone being in the spirit of the law would lead to much lower crime rates.

# CHAPTER TWELVE

# CRIME AND CRIME PREVENTION

The cost of crime is quite high. We should have systems that minimize the cost of crime. When we speak of minimizing the cost of crime, we should address the total cost of crime, not just the first cost. What is the cost of a crime such as a murder? The cost is huge. Everything from the calculable, such as lost wages, burial costs, police time, court time, and incarceration costs, to the incalculable, such as the fear and terror felt by those who survived the victim.

The lowest possible cost of crime would be achieved when people wouldn't even contemplate crime. The only way this goal can be reached is to raise children in families that disdain crime, where the parents teach their children about the moral reasons why crime is not acceptable, and they model noncriminal behavior. This can only happen when the child is a valued member of the family and has the ability to learn in an educational setting and by participating in meaningful work.

How do you raise people who might contemplate committing a crime? Have the children raised by criminals and people who don't respect the moral reasons for not committing crime. Raise children in dysfunctional families, where committing crime might even be part of the child's role in the family. Raise a neglected child, or raise a child in a nonloving situation where the child is not valued. Raise a child in a situation where the only reason the child was born in the first place was so the mother could collect a higher welfare payment. Restrict good educational opportunities, both in formal education and by restricting meaningful employment. Teach children that society owes them something just because they exist.

My local newspaper is the *Minneapolis Star-Tribune*. The January 20, 2002, issue contained a column by Doug Grow, a self-described liberal. The column discussed a study known as The African American Men Project, which was undertaken by Mark Stenglein, a conservative Hennepin County commissioner. Hennepin County encompasses the city of Minneapolis and most of its major suburbs. The gist of the column was that the liberal columnist was pleasantly surprised that a conservative could sponsor such a meaningful study. (The study is available online at www.co.hennepin.mn.us.)

The African American Men Project found that 44 percent of the black males between the ages of 18 and 30 were arrested each year in Hennepin County. The study also stated that 47 percent of these 18- to 30-year-old black men were raised by single mothers, and only 28 percent of these men attending public high school in Minneapolis graduated from high school in four years. I think the arrest rate was the major finding of the study. If this study had been an experiment, then the arrest rate would be the significant experimental outcome. In an experiment, these last two statistics—being raised by a single mother, and the time it took to graduate from high school—would be variables that might affect the experiment's outcome. The study did not say if there was correlation between the arrest rate and being raised by a single mother or between the arrest rate and not graduating in four years.

In the liberal paradigm, there are some obvious answers to this troubling arrest statistic. One answer for this high arrest rate could be that the police department must be racist. Other obvious answers are that the Minneapolis education system must be underfunded, and that the single mothers' welfare payments must not be adequate to raise well-rounded children.

In the conservative paradigm, the cause and effect are much different. Blacks have not always had such a poor arrest record, even in times of much greater perceived prejudice. In the conservative paradigm, the failure of inner-city black society may be traced to the government social programs established in the name of helping the poor. This 44 percent yearly arrest rate would be an indication of black society failure, or at least a portion of black society. When compared to other races, a higher percentage of the total black population was poor at the time of the inception of these government programs. Thus, the results of these programs are likely to show up disproportionately in the black population. In the conservative paradigm, it is believed that whatever negative social path blacks take is soon followed by members of other races.

In this study, I could not find any statistics that would indicate a direct correlation between the participation of the criminals' families in government programs and the arrest rate. Studies undertaken by government officials do not usually look for government to be the source of the problem, so this data is not sought. I would love to have a further study undertaken that examined the family background of all people arrested—not just the blacks arrested—to see the family history with regard to participation in government programs. The Hennepin County study is actually very racist in concept. Instead of trying to identify what the problem is with the 44 percent of the black population that was arrested, the study assumes there is a correlation between crime and race. I would guess that there is a greater correlation between family dependency on government programs and arrest rates than between race and arrest rates.

There was at least one statistic in the study that would suggest high participation in government programs by the population studied. In the Minneapolis School District, children are given free school lunches if the family income is less than 130 percent of the federal poverty level. During the 1997 school year, 8,023 (74.5 percent) of the 10,765 black students within the Minneapolis School District received free lunches. Reduced lunch rates were available to children from families whose income was between 130 and 185 percent of the federal poverty level. An additional 760 children fell within this group, bringing the total to

8,783 (81.6 percent) of 10,765 black children who were either receiving free or subsidized school lunches.

In any case, it's an amazing statistic: 44 percent of the black male population between the ages of 18 and 30 are arrested each year. If anything highlights the failure of government programs to cure a social ill, this would be the statistic to use. I believe the combination of all kinds of government programs has led to this terrible failure of public policy. In my opinion, government policies that create the social conditions leading to this high arrest rate include the minimum wage law, laws that will not allow children to work until they reach a certain age, welfare laws that make it financially advantageous not to have fathers in the home and to have additional fatherless children, food stamps, subsidized housing, and poor-quality public schools.

Advancement in society is a multigenerational issue. The successful immigrants who come to our country have always advanced in stages. The new immigrants take whatever jobs are available and start gaining skills that are valuable in the free market. The new immigrants may never be employed in the better jobs that actually fit their abilities, but they are willing to take lesser jobs to help the next generation. The members of the next generation work hard in school and learn from their parents' experiences and become quite successful. Nowhere in these success stories is the government relied on—even if government programs may occasionally be used. The only thing relied upon is families.

The wealthy in our country live in a free-market economy, and they do well even though much of their wealth is taken from them through taxation. The poor in our society live in a socialist society, and do poorly even though they have low tax rates and may even be subsidized by the government. For the poor, the government is the provider for the family. Statistically, boys living in a home with a man other than their father are much more likely to get into trouble when compared to boys living in a home with their father. In the case of the single mother living on welfare, the other man in her life is the government. The government makes a lousy father.

In the conservative paradigm, the poor take the brunt of the liberal programs' unintended damaging effects. The poor live in a socialist society where they are dependent on the government for food, medical care, housing, schooling, and protection from crime.

The false promise of socialism is a trap that is easy to fall into. The premise of socialism is that those with much wealth will willingly supply some of their wealth to those who have little, at no cost to either party. In actuality both parties suffer in the socialist system. I know of no large-scale socialist system that is voluntary. The people whose money is taken away feel that it was stolen from them, and that the recipients are therefore living on stolen funds. For further discussion of this topic, please see chapter eight on the fairness of taxes for transfer payments.

Let's get specific about government programs that are aimed at helping the poor but have exactly the opposite of the intended effect. For example, look at the minimum wage law. In the liberal paradigm, there is a minimum amount of money that a person needs in order to survive, and to work for less than a certain amount of money is considered demeaning. Therefore, a law was passed to prevent people from making less than this demeaning amount of money.

When I think of the minimum wage law, I think of an old saying that my dad often quoted: "You may ignore the law of supply and demand, but you cannot repeal the law of supply and demand." The liberal politicians disrupted the marketplace and set the wage rate at a level where some people's cost to an employer exceeded the value of employing them. If the cost of employing someone is greater than the return the employer will receive from hiring that person, there is no incentive to hire the person with low-value job skills.

In the conservative paradigm, the minimum wage has had a detrimental effect on teenage unemployment. Conservatives have stated a number of statistics that illustrate the detrimental effect the minimum wage law has had on the poor, and especially, the minority poor. I tried to find this information, but wasn't successful. I did find some interesting statistics at the Bureau of Labor Statistics (http://stats.bls.gov) that listed the unemployment rates for teenagers aged 15 to 17 by family income and race.

Teenagers from the wealthiest families had relatively low unemployment rates: whites, 12.5 percent; blacks, 11.1 percent; and Hispanics, 11.8 percent. I think this is an interesting statistic. Even more interesting is the comparison to the teenage unemployment rate of the lowest income families. The unemployment rate for the low income families were whites, 26.6 percent; blacks, 45.0 percent; and Hispanics, 32.4 percent.

In experimental work you may end up with data that may be attributable to more than one factor. This data is known as confounded data. These teenage unemployment statistics are confounded statistics that beg for further research. Questions that come to my mind include: Are the wealthy families' teenage unemployment rate low because the wealthy families of all races realize the value of work and therefore pressure their teenagers to get jobs? Are the wealthy teenagers wiser than their poorer counterparts and realize the value of jobs and therefore seek employment? Do the wealthy families live in areas where jobs are more plentiful? Are the poor less skilled or less dependable so employers are not as willing to hire them?

It seems that there is a definite correlation between work and wealth found in these unemployment numbers. Does this surprise anyone? In the conservative paradigm, the minimum wage law is an impediment to the poor finding employment. This impediment should be removed. The current minimum wage law is highly unfair to the poor because the poor need to enter the work force if they are ever going to get out of poverty and further proceed down the path to becoming wealthy.

In the conservative paradigm, work has value much greater than the wage being paid. The total value of the job is the wage, plus the value of on-the-job learning, plus the value to other potential employers of demonstrated responsibility shown by a dependable work record, and the value gained in dealing with other people such as customers and fellow employees. The unemployed not only lose income, but they also do not receive the added personal value that is gained from employment. Work also serves the purpose of providing a productive outlet for a person's time and energy. If you are not working, your time will be used in some other capacity. The old saying "The devil finds work for idle hands" properly reflects the view of work held by those in the conservative paradigm.

If young people are not engaged in meaningful employment, then they are much more likely to be headed for trouble. If young people wish to be employed, but laws prevent this, then they may end up entering the illegal or underground economy, which will further aid them in finding trouble.

The liberal answer to unemployment is even more government involvement by establishing government job programs. The conservative answer is for the government to repeal the minimum wage law and age limitations on employment, and then get out of the way. The problem with government-created job programs is that they often do not meet an economic need. The people filling these jobs are not stupid. They know the jobs are not fulfilling an economic need and that the real reason for their employment is to meet a government objective. The government wants these people to be employed, which means that they can do just about anything and not lose their jobs.

We are all aware of multiple government programs intended to help the poor. I do not intend to take the time to address each program individually, but suffice it to say that, as the arrest record in the Hennepin County study indicates, these programs are not working. The poor need to participate in a vibrant market without government interference. The poor need to be lawful, to live in the spirit of the law, and those who are not lawful need to be removed from society. There is no other answer that I am aware of that will effectively reduce high crime rates.

# CHAPTER THIRTEEN

# UNJUST GOVERNMENT-CREATED WEALTH TRANSFERS

Conservatives often address government interference in the marketplace and how this government interference affects the poor. We conservatives address things such as the minimum wage law and work restrictions based on age. However, I believe the conservative message of government interference in the marketplace too often fails to address the government interference that leads to riches.

Milton Friedman makes the argument that the only monopolies that exist have been allowed to exist by the government. An example of a government-granted monopoly is the monopoly power government grants to utilities. I know of no free market monopolies.

I have huge admiration for Bill Gates, the founder of Microsoft. He ventured off to college, but quit right away to follow his passion. Following this passion led him to become the richest man in America. Has he accomplished this amazing feat without the aid of government?

The writers of the Constitution, wishing to foster invention and progress, gave Congress the ability to create laws that would protect ideas and inventions, ensuring that inventors would reap at least some of the profits from their innovations. Section 8 of Article I, which defines some of the powers of Congress, states that Congress can pass laws to "promote the Progress of Science and useful Arts, by securing for limited Times to Authors and Inventors the exclusive Right to their respective Writings and Discoveries."

As I understand it, the reason patent law exists is to give the inventor a monopoly on the invention. This monopoly has value, as any monopoly has value, and can assist the inventor in securing the financial backing necessary to bring his or her invention to market.

Large and very capable companies have been granted patents. I believe that the laws protecting ideas and inventions have been used by these large companies to control and increase market share. Should these large and very capable companies be able to fully use this government protection? I say no. I think Microsoft is a prime example. Microsoft developed the trademarked product, known as the Windows operating system, and has sold millions of copies. This was revolutionary technology. Great. Give the company protection for a certain amount of time, or until a certain amount of profit has been made, or until a certain company market capitalization level has been reached, and then drop or reduce the protection. I don't pretend to have a total solution to this, but it is hard to compare the current Microsoft with the struggling individual inventor envisioned by the authors of the Constitution. Let Microsoft compete in an open market, and let the consumer prices of currently government-protected products drop.

The patent and trademark rules were established to protect the individual from being preyed on by companies, not to keep large corporations protected from the marketplace. The way the system is today, the big companies use patent law to their advantage. Shouldn't these large entities be able to compete in the marketplace without government help? Is it the intent of government to guarantee that a company that is making money hand over fist be allowed to continue making this money at the expense of the consumer?

A further issue I have is that this government-granted patent protection for large and powerful corporations actually stymies economic progress.

It's my belief that companies go through a life cycle. Companies are founded by people who are innovative and who bring new ideas and products to the marketplace. At this early stage of development the companies are generating jobs and producing much wealth. As the company matures, the founders eventually retire or move on to other challenges. The maturing company slowly becomes more bureaucratic and led by people who are good at corporate politics and not so good at innovation. These companies generate few new jobs and create minimal new wealth.

I'll use automobiles as an example once again. The automobile industry was shaken and forever changed by the foreign competition in the 1970s and 1980s. The success of the foreign companies is often attributed to many factors, but one factor that I have never seen mentioned is that the founders of the foreign car companies were still intimately involved with their businesses, unlike the larger and more bureaucratic domestic car companies.

The government should support a system that rewards wealth creation. If patents are used to restrict this formation of wealth through the support of existing business bureaucracies, then the patent system should be revised.

Another concern I have with unjust wealth transfers has to do with the shear size of the government. With the government being the colossal size that it is and with the amount of our national wealth that it controls, it would seem to be a system ripe for political favors. There is an old political saying that I have heard originating in Mexico. "It is a poor politician that remains a poor politician." How many people have become wealthy not only through employment by the government, but also through government contracts, land swaps, mining and timber deals, and who knows what else? When government is spending my money, it will not oversee the spending of that money as carefully as I would.

Another way government creates wealth for some groups at the expense of other groups is to allow certain professions to control their own numbers and then legally restrict the practice to these professionals. The law of supply and demand states that if you limit the supply the price will increase. Restricting entrance into a profession will increase the salaries of these restricted professions. For example, if there are areas that are not adequately served by doctors, nurses, and pharmacists—such as small towns and inner cities—then in my opinion there are not enough people in these professions. In all of these cases, there are more people wanting to join these professions than there are openings available to train people in the profession. The numbers are not controlled by ability, but by the ability to get into the programs necessary to become one of these professionals. Does this make any sense?

# CHAPTER FOURTEEN

# BASIC ECONOMICS

Economics is a huge subject and I only intend to discuss it in brief.

Most liberals and conservatives refer to the economic system that favors free markets and minimal government economic intervention as capitalism. The liberal view of capitalism is that the rich have access to capital and are thus capable of building ever-increasing wealth with this capital. At a minimum, the last decades disproved this notion of capitalism. A free-market economy needs capital, but from what I have seen, ideas are much more valuable than capital. I think our economic system is incorrectly called capitalism. I prefer to call the optimum economic system the free-market system.

I cannot think of a modern company that has been successful only because of its ability to raise capital. There are many examples of companies with great ideas that have outperformed older, more established companies with access to capital. Microsoft grew from an idea of a teenage college dropout to one of the world's largest corporations, with minimal initial capital. Wal-Mart is another example of a business that did not have the capital of its larger rivals. The basic business idea behind Wal-Mart was to create a retailer that knew to the item what was selling and what wasn't selling. Wal-Mart's success was based on implementing a system to gather this knowledge and to do an outstanding job of inventory control. Toyota, which twenty years ago paled in size compared to the General Motors, Chryslers, and Fords of the world, has become one of the world's premier automobile producers. Toyota accomplished this by doing an outstanding job in many different areas, including running fractional experimentation and establishing superior inventory control. The automobile industry is very capital intensive. Toyota's ability to grow as it has over the past decades shows the value of ideas.

In the conservative paradigm, wealth is created by work. The more workers, raw materials, machinery, and ideas, the greater the wealth that will be produced. In the conservative paradigm, the people who are most valuable to a society are the people who produce much wealth and consume little of that produced wealth. The remaining wealth is then available for a wide range of things, such as medical research, education, charity, capital expenditures, housing, and so on.

In the liberal paradigm, there is a limited amount of wealth and the primary job of economics is to determine how to fairly divide this limited amount of wealth. In the liberal paradigm, there are wealthy people who control capital and there are workers who have been taken advantage of by the wealthy. Liberals most value the politicians who take the wealth from the wealth holders and then fairly distribute this wealth to the less fortunate.

In the liberal paradigm, there is a great concern about jobs. The liberal wants the government and our economic system to create jobs. This job creation will lead to workers spending money, which will in turn create more jobs. Everyone employed will get some of the nation's limited wealth and they will be content.

In the conservative paradigm, there is a wish to create wealth. Work without generating wealth is a waste. The wealth generated by productive work will allow greater resources to be allocated for more wealth creation, and a shrinking percentage of the wealth created will go to provide the basic necessities of life.

I recently heard a story about Milton Friedman visiting India, which highlights this difference between the creation of wealth and the creation of jobs. He saw a group of men digging a ditch using hand shovels.

He asked his escort why they didn't use a much more efficient backhoe to do the job. The Indian escort answered that this was a jobs program, and that if they used a backhoe, all but one of these men would lose their jobs. Milton Friedman wondered, "If it is a jobs program then why don't they issue the men spoons instead of shovels?"

In the conservative paradigm, wide disparities in income are caused by some restriction to entering the marketplace. For instance, there has been an accusation that blacks have been discriminated against in securing home loan financing. My solution to this problem would be for someone to start a business that loaned money to the people who were being discriminated against. This new company could then take market share and profit from the current lenders. This starting of the loan company might be much easier said than done, however. The person trying to establish the home loan company might run into capital requirements established by law, or some other impediment to entering this business. Often, regulated businesses end up using the regulations as a means to keep others from entering their market, creating market distortions that should not exist.

In the liberal paradigm, income disparities are attributed to marketplace failure, which requires government intervention to correct.

In a free market, no one is paid to keep track of others. The law of supply and demand rules the marketplace. There is little enforcement cost. In nonfree markets, laws of men rule the marketplace. Huge enforcement costs are associated with these nonfree markets. Compare the standards of living in free-market economies to the standards of living in non-free-market economies and you will be able to see what the total cost of market manipulation is—and this cost is extremely high.

*The Wall Street Journal* annually publishes the results of a study by the Heritage Foundation entitled the Index of Economic Freedom. I think this is a great concept for a study. I have previously discussed the power of experimentation. This study basically takes already existing data on economic freedom and makes this information the variable data of an experiment, showing how the amount of economic freedom affects any number of outcomes, such as the country's standard of living.

In the 2002 Index of Economic Freedom study, 156 countries were rated. Afghanistan, Sudan, Democratic Republic of Congo, Angola, and Somalia were so lawless that they were considered impossible to analyze in this study.

The Heritage Foundation's study on the relative economic freedom of countries highlights the cost of market intervention. Compare Hong Kong, Singapore, New Zealand, Estonia, Ireland, Luxembourg, the Netherlands, the United States, Australia, Chile, the United Kingdom, Denmark, Switzerland, and Finland—countries listed as free in the study—with Iran, Laos, Cuba, Libya, Iraq, and North Korea—countries rated as most repressed. By any measurement, the countries listed as free are much more successful. People try to immigrate to the free countries. People try to leave the countries listed as repressed. The repressed people may not be able to vote in elections, but they often vote with their feet by leaving the repressive countries, oftentimes at great risk.

We often think of the Middle East's on-going problems as caused by religion and culture. The problems could well be economic. The Middle Eastern countries were rated as follows in the 2001 Heritage Foundation study:

Countries rated as free: None

Countries rated as mostly free:

- Bahrain—tied at 15th with Canada
- United Arab Emirates—tied at 23rd with Cyprus and Iceland
- Israel—tied at 43rd with Costa Rica
- Jordan—tied at 45th with seven other countries including France, Poland, and Panama
- Kuwait—tied at 53rd with Peru

All other countries of the Middle East were rated as mostly unfree or repressed. Saudi Arabia, the largest exporter of oil in OPEC, was ranked in a tie for 72nd place along with Uganda, Mauritius, and the Dominican Republic. Turkey, who has been a valued military partner of the United States, was tied for 105th place in the ranking along with Indonesia and Moldova.

In economically free countries you are in control of your life. If you make yourself more valuable to the economy, you will reap the rewards of that effort. In nonfree countries you are not in control of your life. No matter what you do in the nonfree economy your advancement will be in jeopardy. This leads to the nonfree countries having very frustrated, angry, and easily manipulated people.

In the conservative paradigm, we agree with the late Friederich Hayek in his book *The Road to Serfdom* in that we equate free markets with individual freedom. Freedom is equated with the ability to pursue happiness. A secondary value of this freedom is the ability to create wealth and retain it. A corollary would be in the planning of a vacation journey. Much of the fun of a vacation is in the planning, the anticipation, and the unexpected discoveries we happen by on our vacation journey. The destiny of our economic journey is happiness, and if we happen by wealth on this journey, then great. If we don't happen by wealth it is still quite a trip.

In the conservative paradigm, the world has run a huge uncontrolled experiment. In this experiment the variable is government burden on the people, and the outcome of this experiment is the country's standard of living. In the conservative paradigm, the results of this huge experiment tell us that the less the government burdens its people the higher the people's standard of living.

Another conservative view is that we are all consumers. Free markets best serve consumers. Businesses approach government in a number of ways to justify why their particular market needs protection or a government subsidy or tax breaks. The only reason why the government should be concerned about markets is if that business is required for national security reasons, and even then the claims of need for government protection are usually dubious. A costly program that benefits the few at the expense of the many can be seen in the sugar markets. The U.S. government restricts the importation of sugar. The world price of sugar is about $.07 per pound and the domestic price is about $.20 per pound. This restriction on trade costs you, as a consumer of sugar, $.13 for every pound of sugar you consume. The U.S. sugar industry gets the $.13. The foreign producers lose market share to more inefficient domestic producers. You, as a consumer of sugar, lose.

An added note about the sugar industry: After writing the above paragraph, the *Minneapolis StarTribune* reprinted an editorial from the *Los Angeles Times* about the makers of Lifesavers. The Lifesaver company uses 113 tons of sugar per day. The company was unable to buy low-cost sugar from international markets. This cost the company roughly $29,380 per day. Kraft Foods, which owns Lifesavers, decided to move the Lifesaver company to Quebec from Michigan to save money on the purchase of sugar. Do you think this is what the politicians had in mind when they restricted the importation of sugar?

For a deeper understanding of economics from the conservative point of view, I suggest Thomas Sowell's book *Basic Economics: A Citizen's Guide to the Economy.*

# CHAPTER FIFTEEN

# MILITARY DRAFT

As a result of the September 11, 2001, terrorist attack, there has been talk of reinstating the draft to include, among other duties, homeland protection. In my view, there is only one instance when a country should have to resort to a military draft. This would be if a country were completely insolvent and unable to pay the price required to recruit soldiers.

The first war I remember was Vietnam. I believe the war was unpopular among our soldiers. One reason the Vietnam War was unpopular with the solders was that there was no clear objective of what we were trying to accomplish. I don't think there is anything as demoralizing as not understanding the moral reason for which you might have to die. Another reason the Vietnam War was unpopular with the soldiers was that they were not allowed to defeat the enemy. From what I have gathered from Korean War veterans, the Korean War was a similar demoralizing war.

Soldiers were not terribly excited about fighting in the Vietnam War, and not enough soldiers were enlisting, so the government was faced with a choice. The government could withdraw from the war.

The government could change the strategy of the war. The government could raise the wage rate for soldiers. The government could institute a draft. It was no surprise that the government leaders of that time chose to use the draft.

Implementing the draft meant that the government would not have to change its policies or increase the soldiers' pay to a level that would attract additional enlistees. This led to yet another reason why the war was not popular among the soldiers. The soldiers and their families were really the only ones asked to make any sacrifices during the Vietnam War. It must have been strange. You could be a soldier on leave, playing on a Southern California beach and literally, twenty-four hours later, be in a Vietnam rice paddy being shot at. Had the government been forced to change its policies because of its inability to recruit enough soldiers, perhaps the outcome of the Vietnam War could have been different. I look at low recruitment levels as an indication of what young people think of government policy. We have some brave people in America. They will fight if the cause is just. Low recruitment is a reflection on the operation of our military and our foreign policy. We shouldn't lose this check and balance in the military labor market by implementing forced enlistment.

If the government had had to raise the soldiers' wages during the Vietnam War, then the U.S. taxpayers would have had to share a little bit more of the soldiers' burden and the soldiers might have been held in higher regard because they were getting paid more. I think this makes a huge difference in soldier morale. A person's pay reflects how his or her job is valued. When a society stoops to drafting soldiers, it is telling them, "We want you to fight and possibly die, but we don't feel you are important enough for us to pay you adequately to undertake this endeavor on your own."

I love Milton Friedman's discussion on this topic. Friedman asks why you never hear of non-military bureaucracies not having enough recruits. Does anyone ever wonder why we don't need a draft to fill these bureaucracies? I assume this is because these bureaucrats are more highly valued by the government powers, and therefore their relative pay is higher. Relatively higher pay means more people want the job.

The conservative believes that the marketplace can even work for soldiers. There are a number of things that stop our leaders from entering into unpopular wars. One of these checks is our soldiers' willingness to enlist. With a draft, this economic check on our politicians' desire to wage war is removed.

# CHAPTER SIXTEEN

# ENVIRONMENTAL POLICY

The conservative environmental paradigm is similar to the liberal environmental paradigm in that both sides believe that the government should take some responsibility for providing people a healthy environment in which to live. Where the liberal and conservative environmental paradigms diverge, however, is in determining who pays for the protection of the environment, what should be mandated to individuals to achieve global environmental goals, and what should be mandated to individuals about their personal environments, such as their homes.

In the liberal paradigm, the scope of what is included in the government's environmental role is huge. The government's environmental duties include such things as protecting endangered species, participating in efforts to reduce global climate change, regulating land usage, and setting standards for gas mileage, housing, toilet water usage, indoor air quality, and so on. The list goes on and on. In the liberal paradigm, civil liberties may be compromised in the name of protecting the environment.

In the conservative paradigm, the government's environmental role is restricted to those things that can cause health problems. This is basically limited to water and air pollution and flood control. In the conservative paradigm, basic liberties come before environmental concerns. An example of how the paradigms differ is seen in the application of the Endangered Species Act. There are people who make their living farming land where endangered species have been found. In carrying out the wishes of Congress, these people have been forced to stop farming their land. In the liberal paradigm, this is what the law requires. In the conservative paradigm, the farmer has lost a basic liberty because the government has in effect taken the farmer's land. The conservative thinks it is the government's right to keep the farmer from farming the land to protect the endangered species, but that the farmer must be reimbursed for the loss of land value and income. We conservatives believe the loss in value of the farmer's land is confiscation by the government, which violates the Fifth Amendment of the Constitution. Article V ends with this wording: ". . . nor shall private property be taken for public use without just compensation."

An entire book could be written on the environment, and I do not wish to do this. I would, however, like to address a few of my issues relating to the environment.

The first issue is global warming. There are a few things tied to the global warming discussion that I find troubling. First, carbon dioxide gas, which is being touted as the major greenhouse gas that is causing the earth to warm, is unbelievably solvent in water. A pint of water will hold about a pint of carbon dioxide gas at one atmosphere of pressure. A soft drink has about this level of carbon dioxide dissolved in it. The oceans can hold unbelievable amounts of carbon dioxide. If there is excess carbon dioxide in the atmosphere it will want to dissolve into rain and other waters such as the ocean. The oceans will absorb the carbon dioxide and marine plants will utilize this carbon dioxide and produce oxygen. If carbon dioxide is too plentiful in the ocean waters, then the carbon dioxide will also drop out of solution as bicarbonate.

An argument that some scientists use to prove that there is a global warming trend is to use historic temperature records at a given location. Temperature is related to the energy in the air, but it is not the measurement of total energy in the air. Air is mostly made up of nitrogen, oxygen, and water vapor. For oxygen and nitrogen, the temperature does reflect the value of energy in the air. The energy in the air owing to the amount of water vapor in the air is highly variable. The energy in the air due to the amount of this variable water quantity is not well represented by temperature.

For example, if an area is drier, its temperature may be higher, but the actual energy in the air may be lower. An example of an area that is hot but has little energy in the air is the desert southwest of the United States. The temperature of the air may be much higher in a southwestern city, such as Santa Fe, than in a location with sometimes tropical weather, such as Miami. The amount of energy in the air in Santa Fe may be much less than in Miami owing to the fact that there is little water vapor in Santa Fe's desert air and much water vapor in Miami's tropical air.

Many people in the desert southwest used to use air conditioners known as swamp coolers. In a swamp cooler, hot, dry air is placed in contact with water. The water evaporates into the hot air, and the energy taken from the hot air to evaporate the water reduces the air stream's temperature while increasing its humidity. This cooling effect caused by the water evaporating into the air stream is similar to the cooling effect you notice when you get out of the water after swimming. The temperature of the water that contacts this dry air approaches what is known as the dew point of the air. The dew point is the temperature to which a mass of air would have to cool to in order for the water vapor in the air stream to condense and thus form dew. The air stream resulting from this contact between the water and the hot, dry air is a cooler and more humid air stream, but an air stream that has the same energy as the hot and dry air stream that initially entered the swamp cooler.

Just south of Jackson, Wyoming, there is a campground that has a geothermally heated pool. The temperature of the water is about 98 degrees Fahrenheit. I was swimming in this pool on a cool and crisp late summer night with perfectly clear skies. The swimming was absolutely beautiful. The warm water and the stunning, star-filled sky made the night one of the most memorable experiences of my life. Getting out of the pool was also a memorable experience. It may have been the coldest experience of my life, and for a lifelong Minnesota resident, that is saying something. When I exited the pool, the temperature of the water remaining on my skin quickly dropped toward the dew point, which was very low in the dry mountain valley air. To say the least, that was a refreshing moment.

Since temperature does not reflect the amount of energy in the air owing to moisture, engineers and scientists use a value called enthalpy, which is the true measure of the total energy in the air. I find it absurd to argue for global warming trends based on small differences in temperature changes over many years, without taking moisture into consideration. If you are trying to prove global warming, the problem with using enthalpy is that there are historical temperature records, but no extensive historical enthalpy records. If there are no historical records of enthalpy, then there is no proof of this value changing.

For the most part, official temperature measurements are taken at airports. The areas around most airports have, over time, become more urbanized. Urbanization leads to locally lower humidity, due to the fact that there is less plant life and natural ground surface area giving up moisture to these environments. As humidity drops for a given air mass, the air mass's temperature will rise.

On a massive scale, this increase in air temperature owing to low humidity is what happened in the Midwest and Great Plains states during the dust bowl years of the 1930s. If you look at the temperature records of the Midwest and the cities of the Great Plains, you will find a large number of record high temperatures during the Dust Bowl years of the 1930s. These record high temperatures were reached because there was so little humidity in the air, allowing the air temperature to rise dramatically.

I wish to present a hypothesis on ice ages and global warming that I have not seen mentioned anywhere. We know that the earth has historically been both much warmer and much cooler than it is today. We also know that the surface of the sea, whether water or ice, controls most of our weather, and that in the lower depths of the sea the water is quite cold everywhere, even in the tropics. Warm water is less dense than cold water, so the warm water floats on top of the cold water.

Having this warm water at the surface results in the earth's weather being comparatively warm. My hypothesis is that the earth slowly warms under normal conditions. I conclude that this warming takes place because the location where I am presently writing was once under hundreds of feet of ice. We have obviously warmed since the last ice age, and it is equally obvious that man could not have had much of an effect on this.

If some major event were to cause the mixing of the upper and lower waters of the sea, then the ocean surface would become relatively cold. For example, let's say that the first 100 feet of the ocean surface has a temperature of 80 degrees and the next 1,000 feet has a temperature of 40 degrees. If you mixed this column of water you would end up with 1,100 feet of 44-degree water.

If this mixing of lower and upper ocean waters were to take place, our weather would cool appreciably because the surface of the ocean would become much cooler. Cold sea surface waters would lead to less water vapor being released into the earth's atmosphere, which would lead to additional cooling because water vapor is one of the most significant of the earth's greenhouse gases. This cooling of the surface waters of the sea would keep warm ocean currents, such as the Gulf Stream, from developing and warming the polar regions. The lack of ocean currents would lead to extremely cold weather toward the poles. This cold weather at the poles could provide the necessary conditions for an ice age to develop.

What kind of an event could cause such mixing of the ocean waters? I would guess that often mentioned meteor impacts would have a large effect on the earth, with ocean mixing being just one of the results. I saw an interesting example of one possible such event on a PBS program about the Mediterranean Sea. The program argued that at one time the entrance to the Mediterranean Sea had been sealed at Gibraltar, and the water entering it from other sources was not great enough to keep the sea filled. The evidence for this historically lower level was the discovery at the mouth of the Nile River of a deep river channel that extended far out into the Mediterranean. This river channel could only have formed if the level of the sea had at one time been much lower. At some point in the world's history, the blockage at Gibraltar opened, allowing ocean waters to flood into the Mediterranean Sea. My guess is that this rush of water would have caused a dramatic up-welling of cooler ocean waters from the depths of the Atlantic Ocean, leading to much cooler Atlantic Ocean surface waters.

Considering the historical data pointing to previous warm and cold periods on earth, if global warming is taking place now, it may be a natural rather than a man-made occurrence. If global warming is happening, man's influence may be playing a role. At this point, I believe it is impossible to know whether or not mankind is having a significant influence on the earth's climate.

Conservatives' concern about the global warming issue is taxation. Politicians realize that the populace will not stand for any new personal income taxes—except for those taxes levied on someone else. A fossil fuel tax would meet all of the politicians' tax criteria. The tax would be hidden from the voters by being levied against businesses, and it would be done in the name of helping the environment. Life doesn't get any better for politicians than when they are able to increase funding for the government under the guise of environmental concern.

The second environmental issue I wish to address is radon gas. I think it was about 1990 when we suddenly found out that we're all going to get lung cancer if we didn't do something about radon gas. Radon gas is a naturally occurring radioactive gas produced underground by the decay of radioactive materials. This gas may seep into buildings and will dissolve into groundwater.

How did radon gas become a concern of health officials? It was noticed that uranium miners had a higher incidence of lung cancer than the general public. It was also known that the mines had increased levels of radon gas. If a correlation could indeed be established between radon gas and higher levels of lung cancer, which I'm suspecting can be readily made, then I would say that the miners should be warned and increased safety measures should be implemented in the mines. Here is the part I have trouble with. It is also known that some radon gas enters homes. To extrapolate the mine conditions to home conditions and then scare the public with the resulting number of estimated deaths is just plain bad science and bad public policy.

I happened across a map showing the areas of the country that had high levels of radon gas. This interested me because some of the areas with the highest levels of radon gas were my home state of Minnesota and one neighboring state in particular, North Dakota. I also know that these two states have some of the highest life expectancies in our country. My question is, if radon is bad for you, why do the areas with the highest radon levels have the people with the longest life expectancy? If you were running an experiment and the variable was the amount of radon gas in a given geographical area and the outcome was the longevity of people living in those areas, then it would seem that adding radon gas to homes should be required. I'm not advocating this, but the correlation between longevity and radon gas levels should be explored before the government adds huge costs to the housing industry with no data confirming that radon gas actually is a health problem at the levels found in homes.

My last environmental issue concerns wetlands. The beauty of this wetland topic is that it involves all of the following:

- Bad science.
- Tyranny of the majority over the minority group of wetland owners.
- Increased housing prices.
- Increased health risks.
- Loss of wetlands.

I have an interest in water quality, and my wife and I own some property that is about 80 percent wetlands. Wetlands may be beneficial to some watersheds. Wetlands may accomplish the following:

- Act as a reservoir for absorbing and holding excessive runoff caused by heavy rain and snow melt.
- Act as a source for recharging groundwater aquifers.
- Allow for the silt in silt-laden waters to settle out of suspension.

- Growth of plants within the wetland filters out nutrients that could allow for harmful algae blooms further downstream.

Wetlands may also cause some problems including the following:

- Over time, wetlands tend to become acidic and may acidify waters flowing through them. Most marine plants and animals prefer slightly basic (opposite of acidic) water.

- The emergent plants of a wetland that filter out nutrients from the water eventually die and fall back into the wetland. The plants then decay and cause low-dissolved oxygen conditions. The decaying plants release nutrients back into the water and these nutrients may lead to destructive algae blooms further downstream.

- Water within a wetland may often become devoid of oxygen, which is the condition that allows disease-carrying mosquitoes to flourish. This happens because most predators that prey on mosquito larvae need dissolved oxygen to survive.

I believe the government (although I'm not sure it should be the federal government) has an appropriate concern in preventing floods and in recharging aquifers, but the rest of the wetland agenda is the government choosing a particular form of water management. The government plan is no better or no worse than any other plan. It is a choice. I do not understand the reasoning as to why the government is dictating their choice to the landowners.

For example, let's say that the government has determined that there is a need for 10 acre feet of water retention capacity within a segment of a watershed. This could be accomplished by having 10 acres of land with 1 foot of water depth, or 1 acre of land with 10 feet of water depth. Which is a better means of holding the 10-acre-feet of water? Why is the government telling me how to retain the 10-acre-feet of water?

The government has adopted a no-wetland-loss policy and, in keeping with a government that disregards our constitution's Fifth Amendment, has forced landowners to comply with the policy. The government has forced its view on a small minority of landowners who do not have the political clout to do anything about it. Isn't this use of government force the definition of tyranny? This enforcement results in loss of freedom to the landowner at no cost to the people as a whole. In the conservative paradigm, this is an unjust action. If the government is going to use the land, then the government should pay for the usage.

In my own situation, six government agencies have taken an interest in my property. These government agencies are my township, my county, a state agency known as a watershed district, my state department of natural resources, the federal soil and water people, and the Army Corps of Engineers. All people for whom salaries, equipment and fuel are paid for through my taxes that regulate me in my use of land that I own. My land has been limited to the amount of housing that may be constructed on this site because of wetlands restrictions. As a land-owner I have no recourse. If the government told me that I had to have the ability to retain a certain amount of runoff, I could live with that. If the government told me that the quality of the water leaving my land could not be degraded, I could live with that. What the government tells me is that I now own what amounts to private parkland. I am unable to utilize my own land. Thanks a lot.

I would also wish to point out that this loss of building eligibility has nothing to do with filling the wetland or doing anything else detrimental to the wetland. I could, for instance, raise livestock in this area, which would be much more detrimental to the wetland than building housing on this property. Also this wetland rarely has water on its surface. During most of the year, on what is considered wetland, the land could be walked on without getting your feet wet. My county has restricted the use of any wetlands or land within 75 feet of a wetland from being considered in calculating lot size. Now, 75 feet may not sound like much, but if you have a round one-acre wetland, then restricting the wetland, plus 75 feet around the wetland, ends up restricting more than 2.67 acres of land.

You may be saying to yourself that this is a selfish argument on my part because I have lost wealth from the decreased value of the land. I make the argument that I lose wealth, but also the home buyers in my area lose wealth because of the reduction in building eligibility that leads to high housing prices. This, in turn, hurts the poor. This concept of high housing prices caused by government-created housing restrictions is explored in a paper by Harvard economist Edward Glaeser and Joseph Gyourko of the Wharton School of the University of Pennsylvania. The paper was undertaken on behalf of the National Bureau of Economic Research (http://post.economics.harvard.edu/hier/2002papers/HIER1948.pdf.). The paper's findings were summarized by Virginia Postrel in an article entitled, "Housing Costs Vary Between 'Red' 'Blue' America" in the April 6, 2002, issue of the *Minneapolis StarTribune*. In this article, the economists found that housing prices were artificially increased when the right to build is limited by government. Basic economics tell us that if the supply of something is limited for a given demand the price will rise. High cost housing ultimately hurts the poor. The same government that is supposed to be a champion of the people becomes the tyrant over these people, unnaturally limiting the people's housing choices.

The result of current wetland law is the devaluation of wetlands and of lands near wetlands. In the conservative paradigm, if something is devalued you get less of it. The Farm Belt has millions of acres of land that have been drained for agricultural purposes and that could easily become restored wetlands. Why would anyone restore wetlands if the restoration results in decreased value to the landowner? Again, using the wetlands I own as an example, the government agencies all tell me they would like to see a wetland on my property. I would also like to have a wetland on my property, with this feature being one of the main reasons I purchased the property initially. Since the government has created a situation where a wetland will have a negative economic impact, I, as a wetland owner, will do everything I can legally do to minimize the size of the wetland on my property, the exact opposite of that which all the interested parties would like to see. Instead of the government forcing landowners to comply with their wishes, it seems to me, that government agencies wishing to keep or reestablish wetlands would be working on ways to make the wetlands economically more valuable, giving landowners economic incentive to retain and restore wetlands.

The last item concerning wetlands is one of public health. The United States has historically been relatively free from serious mosquito-transmitted diseases. This situation has changed for the worst with the introduction of the virus causing West Nile viral encephalitis or meningitis. This virus was first noticed in New York and has now spread as far south as Florida and as far west as Wisconsin. The virus is carried by a number of mosquito species, including the common house mosquito. This information and the extent of the problem may be reviewed at www.ci.nyc.ny.us/, and search using "West Nile virus."

As far as water quality is concerned, one of the best thing you could do is to have the water flow through a bed of emergent plants. The emergent plant material would have to be removed periodically to keep dead plant material from affecting the water quality. The only negative point about doing this water treatment would be that the water may become relatively warm because the emergent plant bed needs a shallow water depth.

Warm water with little dissolved oxygen to support the life of mosquito predators are common in wetlands owing to the shallowness of the water and the large amount of decaying plant material. A physical property of warm water is that it is unable to hold much dissolved oxygen. Most water-dwelling mosquito predators find themselves in a deadly catch-22 situation. The higher the water temperature, the less oxygen that water can hold, but the higher the water temperature the more active the predator needs to be, which increases the predator's oxygen demands. This situation leads ultimately to the death of the mosquito predators. The mosquito is able to survive these low-dissolved oxygen conditions because the mosquito larvae are able to breathe atmospheric oxygen through a tube, which later becomes the probe used by the female mosquito to withdraw the mosquito victim's blood. Mosquito predators that utilize gills, or that absorb oxygen directly through their skin, cannot survive in these dead, oxygen-deficient waters. This is because of the low oxygen conditions and the increased need for oxygen caused by the warm water.

From a public safety standpoint these oxygen-depleted waters should be drained to bodies of water that have sufficient levels of oxygen to support the mosquito's predators or the waters should be aerated, a process that adds dissolved oxygen to water. Another solution to this would be to treat all mosquito hatching areas to prevent the mosquito larvae from hatching, but my experience is that these efforts are not going to be satisfactory.

Which of the six government agencies that regulate the wetland that we own is going to take credit for the ensuing sickness and possible death that is going to take place due to this mosquito-borne disease? I am thankful that I at least live in an area of the country without the more serious disease of malaria, but I am still very concerned about the West Nile virus.

I'll wander here a little before ending this discussion. DDT (dichlorodiphenyltrichloroethane) has been vilified by environmentalists, and environmentalists are pushing for the worldwide ban on the manufacture and distribution of DDT. Jane Orient, a medical doctor, wrote an editorial entitled *DDT and Malaria* that may be found at www.heartland.org, searching on "DDT." Her article argues against the banning of DDT; it states that there are annually 300 to 500 million new cases of malaria worldwide, leading to three million deaths, mostly among children. DDT is the least damaging, most cost-effective pesticide to be used against the mosquito that carries this terrible disease. Annually having three million dead children from a disease boggles the mind. How can we as people not fight against the disallowing of the use of the one potent weapon these poor people have to use against the mosquito?

CHAPTER SEVENTEEN

# HEALTH POLICY

In the liberal paradigm, health care is a basic right. Because health care is a basic right, government should, ideally, run the entire medical system, which would be accomplished by nationalizing the health care industry. By taking over health care, the government would be able to guarantee the provision of this basic right to all people. If nationalizing the health care system is not an option, the government must at least make sure the system is safe, and this is accomplished through the government's regulation of health care.

In the conservative paradigm, government involvement will lead to less than optimal results in any business, even one as important as health care. As health care currently functions, government is already too deeply involved. Because of this involvement, health care is more expensive and less progressive than it would be otherwise. A story of this government involvement follows.

Starting a business has always been a dream of mine. In my spare time I try to think up inventions and new business ideas. A number of years ago, I signed up for a graduate course at the University of Minnesota. The goal of the class was to bring together people with business ideas or inventions and people who were pursuing their

Master of Business Administration (MBA) degree. The idea was to have the MBA student help the entrepreneur write a business plan. I had a number of business ideas and inventions, so I signed up for the class.

One very interesting aspect of this class was that guest entrepreneurs were invited to speak. The guest entrepreneurs would describe everything that was entailed in bringing their businesses or ideas to fruition. These entrepreneurs ranged from people who had started successful businesses to people who were just taking their products to market, to people who were still prototyping their products. Some of these entrepreneurs were highly successful millionaires and some were trying to figure out how to make it financially through the next day.

One person who spoke to the class was a medical doctor who had worked on a medical device. A fellow doctor who had performed autopsies on past angioplasty patients had found scarring on the cadavers' artery walls. (Angioplasty is the mechanical opening of a clogged artery. This procedure is usually accomplished by inserting a catheter through an artery in the groin area and running the catheter up to the heart through the artery.) Occasionally, the catheter used during an angioplasty procedure punctured the patients' artery wall, which resulted in what the doctor described as a major medical problem for the patient. The doctors undertook the effort to improve the catheter to see if artery damage could be eliminated or reduced. They hired an engineer to look at the design of the catheter; the engineer came up with a tip design that would eliminate scarring. This sounded like a great idea to me.

The doctors had done what innovative people do. They noticed a problem, researched the issue, brought in expertise, and solved the problem. Great work! Future heart patients will be better off and the introduction of this revised catheter tip will reduce unneeded surgery and other complications caused by puncturing the artery during the angioplasty procedure. In my view, the only things needed to complete this obvious success story was to find out how much of the market the new device had captured, how much money the doctors were making with their new and improved product, and if the doctors had any new medical problems that they were working on solving.

In the medical products paradigm, this wasn't going to happen so quickly. In order to receive approval to use this new device, the doctors had to give evidence to the Food and Drug Administration (FDA) that this was an improvement to the currently approved device. I do not recall the exact number of angioplasties that had to be done with the new device to be compared to the same number of angioplasties done with the old device, but it was in the thousands. The results of the testing were as expected: much less artery damage and many fewer major medical problems caused by the catheter puncturing the artery wall.

The doctors spoke as if this testing—and the delay in introducing an improved product to the market owing to this required testing—were normal. I was shocked by the thought that people had unnecessarily had a catheter puncture their artery wall because their doctors were now using an old, outdated catheter design. No doubt, there were also a large number of people who had artery scarring because the new product wasn't allowed to come onto the market until testing was complete.

I compare this approval process to a fictional car inventor. The inventor builds a car and finds after driving the car that he or she should have added brakes to the original car design. The inventor decides to add brakes, but is told by some bureaucracy that brakes can't be added without obtaining data showing that brakes will actually prevent crashes. The inventor builds thousands of cars with brakes and thousands of cars without brakes and waits to see what will happen. Obviously, the cars without brakes will have some problems. Is statistical evidence really necessary to prove an obvious design improvement that has sound technical reasoning behind the change?

The original catheter did not need to have the design of the tip approved by the government, but since the design was previously established, any change, even an obvious product improvement, needed government approval before implementation. How heartless can a system be?

This was just one medical device that I happened to hear about because I happened to be in this class. How many items like this exist? I remember reading an article in *The Wall Street Journal* about the about the number of heart attacks that led to the unnecessary deaths of patients while the FDA was approving a drug called TPA. The numbers were amazingly high, but dead people ask no questions. How would most people ever find out about the deaths caused by delays in the approval of a drug? I do not want the FDA bureaucracy intervening in my medical marketplace. My well-being is not as important to the FDA bureaucracy as it is to me.

The cost of drug and equipment development owing to regulation must also be very high. Imagine that you are going to start a company to develop drugs. You have to pay the people to develop the drugs. You have to pay for the building and the support staff. Let's say the business comes up with a new drug after a year of development. You then have to test the drug at all the different levels of testing, and finally you send test results to the FDA for approval. You may not get any revenue from your new drug business for years. This effort would entail a huge financial input. This cost involves the time-cost of money. Present-money is much more valuable than future-money. Investing this valuable present-money to possibly make money in the distant future is not terribly attractive to investors. Who would be willing to make this financial commitment?

I would say that all of the hurdles put in front of a potential drug maker would discourage the introduction of new drugs, which would in turn hurt the patients who would have benefited from the new innovation. Once the approval process is complete, then the drug company has to charge enough to make up for the investment. If the process takes years to develop, the drug maker may never obtain adequate returns on the investment. The consumer of the drug will ultimately pay for all of this, either through high-priced drugs or through poor health caused by the lack of new drugs.

Think of the total cost of the new products being held up in bureaucracy. The cost must be huge. This is a hidden tax, forced on us by government regulation, which the consumers of medical services have to pay. Next time you see an outrageously high medical bill, think of the story of the improved catheter. Next time you hear of someone having problems during a medical procedure, think of the story of the improved catheter.

I believe this government involvement in the drug and medical device marketplace stems from pregnant women taking Thalidomide in the 1950s and 1960s to control morning sickness. This drug caused severe birth defects. But doesn't it seem obvious that you should be very, very careful about giving newer drugs to pregnant women? Although some pregnancies were surely endangered by excessive morning sickness, for many Thalidomide was prescribed even though there was no danger to the fetus or the mother caused by the morning sickness. I oftentimes look at actions from a standpoint of potential loss and potential gain. The potential gain in taking Thalidomide was not to be sick in the morning. The potential loss was the resulting damage done to the fetus. The potential gain seems insignificant to the potential loss in this case.

Isn't it also obvious that you would be less concerned about the testing requirements for drugs given to people who are dying, such as terminally ill cancer patients, who, without intervention, have no chance of survival? The cancer patient's loss from not having curative drugs available is the loss of the cancer patient's life.

Let me expand on this a little further. Suppose a drug was developed for the treatment of terminal cancer. This drug would kill 30 percent of the patients who took the drug, but it would cure the other 70 percent. In order for the drug to work, the drug would have to be taken in the early stages of the terminal cancer. Whose decision should it be to take or not take this drug? A bureaucracy like the FDA would never approve such a drug because of the deaths it would cause. Yet not making the drug available would doom the 70 percent who would have been cured by taking the drug. This decision should be the patient's decision to make. I often tell people I'm pro-choice on almost everything but abortion. The freedom to make medical decisions, especially in the case of terminal disease, is definitely one of the areas where I am pro-choice.

The government is involved in health care at all levels. This involvement includes, but is not limited to, licensing health care workers, approving drugs and medical devices, overseeing hospital accreditation, determining who may sell drugs and to whom they may sell them, and financing our retirees' health care. With this much government involvement, medical costs are naturally high and service is naturally less than optimal.

Completely nationalized systems, such as those of Canada and Great Britain, are facing serious difficulties. I would equate nationalized with socialized. The old saying about socialism being a system where the poverty is equally distributed is very true of these medical systems. These systems end up rationing health care, and this rationing leads to people dying at a greater rate and at an earlier age than they would in a free-market medical system.

# CHAPTER EIGHTEEN

# ABORTION

I am going to change my approach somewhat for the discussion on abortion. I have written and rewritten this chapter many times. During these rewrites I have come to the conclusion that abortion is not a liberal or a conservative issue. I know many liberals who are adamantly opposed to abortion and who do not think that the pro-life position is a conservative position. Most conservatives I know are firmly opposed to abortion, but I do know some who are at least somewhat pro-choice given certain situations. In light of these conflicts, I am going to present the argument mostly in terms of pro-choice and pro-life instead of liberal and conservative positions.

You may ask why, if it is not a conservative or liberal issue, a discussion of abortion is included in this writing. The pro-life stance is no longer welcomed by the liberal political establishment. Only liberals voted to sustain President Clinton's veto of the partial birth abortion bill. The only place that pro-life people are welcome is within conservative circles. My hope is that pro-life liberals will be more open to the rest of the conservative paradigm after having read this book, and I hope they will join with us in our conservative cause.

In the pro-choice paradigm, the mother has supremacy over her body and the body of her unborn child. This supremacy gives the woman the right to have her fetus aborted. The pro-choice people will disagree on whether or not the mother should have this abortion right throughout the entire pregnancy. Most pro-choice people would allow abortion within the first trimester, but many would put no restriction on when an abortion may take place, as proven by the congressional vote to sustain President Clinton's veto of the partial birth abortion bill.

In the pro-life paradigm, unique human life starts at conception. Birth is a milestone. Crawling is a milestone. Walking is a milestone. Starting school, graduating from school, getting a job, getting married, having children, having grandchildren, retiring, and finally death—all are milestones. Birth is not the start of life; it is just a convenient and definite time at which to start measuring age. In the pro-life paradigm, we see no difference between the taking of a life while the baby is living within the mother's womb—one month, four months, or seven months after conception—or the taking of the life ten months after conception when the baby has been out of its mother's womb for a month.

Abortion is a volatile political issue because the paradigms are so radically different. Below I weigh in on the abortion issue.

My son has a genetically related syndrome known as Fragile X. The X and Y chromosome are the sex-determining chromosomes. You get one X chromosome from your mother and either an X or a Y from your father. If you have two Xs, you are female; and if you have an X and a Y, you're male. The other chromosomes in your body are in pairs. You receive one set from your mother and one set from your father. If you have a flaw in one of the chromosomes you've received from one parent, the chromosome received from your other parent will still produce the proteins that the chromosome is supposed to produce, and you may live a fairly normal life. Because males have only one of each of the sex-determining chromosomes, they are much more likely to have problems if there is a flaw on one of them. On my son's X chromosome there is a sequence of DNA that repeats itself an unnatural number of times. As a result of this genetic flaw, this sequence of DNA either produces a protein that the body does not recognize (and therefore cannot use as it would a protein from a normal genetic sequence), or produces no protein at all. Either way, the body ends up lacking a necessary protein.

A common symptom of people with Fragile X is that they acquire extreme attachments to things. In my son's case it is books, tapes, and movies. My son will get to a certain section of a movie or tape and play it over and over and over and over. I bring this up here because of a particular fascination he had with a tape titled *Black Man in America*. I've heard portions of this tape literally thousands of times.

In one section of that tape, a speaker states that the only thing that people who are pro-slavery ask of him is his silence on the subject of slavery, as the justification for slavery cannot stand in the face of open debate. I feel this is also true in the case of abortion. People who are pro-choice never debate the act of abortion.

The pro-choice supporters realize that they cannot win the argument about when a unique individual life begins, so they avoid debating the abortion subject. They make the discussion a debate about women's rights. This was the same tactic that the pro-slavery people used prior to the Civil War. The supporters of slavery debated states' rights, not the rights of the slave. The war was eventually fought over the issue of states' rights versus federal rights. The South could not win the moral argument about slavery, so President Abraham Lincoln was able to use the slave issue to his political advantage in the North, which ultimately resulted in power being gained by the federal government.

A unique human being is created at the moment of conception. I do not believe that there is any possible argument against this. The fact is that this human being has a set of genes that differentiates this individual from the mother. Cells taken from this human being would clearly show that the cells were not the cells of the mother. The cells would also clearly be human. The only difference between the fetus and any of us is our age.

The fetus is an individual human being, genetically quite different from the mother, but very dependent upon the mother to provide the environment necessary for its maturation. With new technology, the uniqueness of the fertilized egg is becoming even more readily apparent.

A fertilized egg may be implanted into the womb of any woman whose body is capable of supplying the needed environment for the fetus to survive. I have heard of women being implanted with their own grandchildren and carrying them through the pregnancy. Assuming the mother is in good health and not subjecting the baby to injurious situations, such as drug abuse, the baby will come out of the womb the same, regardless of who carried the baby to term.

An example of the use of surrogate mothers is seen in the livestock industry. There are female animals whose traits are so valuable that breeders want to pass those genes on to as many animals as possible as quickly as possible. The eggs are removed from the valuable animal, fertilized, and placed into the wombs of other, less valuable animals. This is done to speed the process of breeding as many animals with improved genetics in as short a time as possible.

Let us assume that with the advances in medicine and science an artificial womb could be created to replace a mother's womb. The fertilized egg could be placed in this machine and allowed to mature for the months that the fetus needs to mature to survive outside this artificial womb. Now let me argue that sometime during this period you unplug the machine. Have you not killed the fetus by unplugging the artificial womb? Isn't this killing of the fetus what an abortion is?

In the pro-choice paradigm, I believe that it would be recognized that this fertilized egg is a human being with a unique genetic makeup, but the pro-choice would argue that this human being has yet to attain the status of a person. The fetus at early stages of development has no discernible brain function; to pro-choice people, a being without brain function is not yet a person. From the perspective of at least some of the pro-choice people, the fetus does not attain personhood until it can survive outside the womb. To others, the fetus does not attain personhood until it leaves the womb, even if the fetus is sufficiently developed to survive outside the womb.

The pro-choice argument for allowing abortion during the early stages of fetal development is that if the fetus does not have brain activity then it has not developed enough to be considered human. A pro-choice analogy would be a person who has been in an accident, has lost brain function, and is living in a vegetative state. We pro-life people would concur that it would be acceptable for this brain-dead accident victim in this vegetative state to be removed from life-support equipment. In the case of the fetus, however, it is far from being declared brain dead because the fetus would obviously still be maturing. At the present time, the fetus is unable to survive without the life-support aid of the womb, and may not be showing any detectable brain function, but unlike the vegetative accident victim who will never recover, the fetus will be able to survive without the aid of the life-supporting womb within ninth months at most. No one would ever consider removing life support from an accident victim if there was knowledge that this person would show advanced brain activity in nine months' time.

The last point related to using lack of development as a reason to end the fetal life is one of awareness. If the fetus is insufficiently developed to be aware of dying, is the destruction of this life a moral problem? If someone were to introduce carbon monoxide gas into your home at night while you were sleeping, you would never be aware that you had been murdered. You would have just fallen into a deeper and deeper sleep until being overtaken by death. Even though you were unaware of this happening to you, would you be any less dead? I would consider this a moral problem even if you weren't aware. I consider abortion a moral problem even if the fetus is unaware.

In the pro-life paradigm, the determination of what constitutes a person should not be left to interpretation, for only human death can result. In our own country, slaves—based on their race—were not considered people and were treated accordingly. This treatment could include horrible atrocities or death. In Nazi Germany, many individuals were not considered people, including Jews and the disabled, and these individuals' lives and liberty were taken by the state in the name of bettering society. In the pro-life paradigm of many, life starts at conception, and this life should be allowed to run its natural course until death. Others in the pro-life paradigm believe that government should have the right to execute murderers, but that innocent life is sacred. All of the pro-lifers believe that people should not be given the right to make life-or-death decisions concerning innocent human life.

The laws on the killing of the fetus vary depending on whether the fetus is wanted or not wanted by the mother. Let us assume that a woman has had difficulty becoming pregnant. After years of trying, the woman finally becomes pregnant. This pregnancy is a joy for both the woman and her husband. At five months of pregnancy the woman is involved in a terrible automobile accident, which leads to the death of the fetus. I think we would all agree that this woman and her husband have suffered a terrible loss. My home state of Minnesota recognizes the value of this fetal life and has made it illegal for someone to kill a fetus against the wishes of the mother. You can go to prison for killing a wanted fetus and you can get paid for killing an unwanted fetus. There is something amiss when not all innocent life is treated equally by the law.

The fact that abortion is legal wrongly gives the act of abortion moral standing. For example, if an unmarried woman becomes pregnant against the wishes of the baby's father, or of her own family, and they want her to have her fetus killed, what is her defense if she should wish to carry the baby to term? She will have a hard time claiming religious reasons because she has been religiously immoral by getting pregnant. She has no legal argument because abortion is legal. I pity a woman in this predicament, who may be coerced into taking the life of her baby.

An extreme case of this expectation of abortion recently showed up in the news. A professional football player impregnated a young woman and asked her to terminate the pregnancy. The woman declined and was later killed in a drive-by shooting. The football player was arrested for the murder of this young woman. The young women's right to an abortion had become the expectation of abortion. A woman refused to have a legal abortion and was killed for her choice.

I believe a very large majority of people, both pro-life and pro-choice, would like to see a decrease in the number of abortions performed. At best, abortion is an avoidable medical operation that would be unnecessary if people were responsible for the results of their actions. At worst, it is the willful killing of the baby growing within the woman's womb. There is also data indicating that women who have had pregnancies terminated either naturally or by choice may have a higher incidence of breast cancer, to say nothing of the other potential health problems involved with abortions. Not having an abortion is both physically and emotionally better for the woman than having to go through this procedure.

Also, pregnancy does not just happen. Pregnancy is a result of having sex. The couple makes a human choice to decide to have sex. To consent to have sex should be to consent to the potential results of that decision.

With abortion legal, and with the way insurance and welfare are set up, we anti-abortion people end up paying for what we consider to be an extremely immoral and inhumane act—immoral because of the destruction of life, and inhumane because of the callous disregard for the fetus's pain. I personally cannot think about the actual act of abortion without almost becoming physically ill.

The courts have intervened and somehow found a right to abortion in our Constitution. This is a very interesting reading of our Constitution. I read our Constitution and find no opinion on allowing abortion to take place or not take place. I believe you could make the argument that since the fetus is human, it should be granted the full protection of the law, just like any other human. In my conservative paradigm, if an issue is not addressed in the Constitution, then the states are supposed to deal with that issue. I believe the federal courts had no business getting involved on the side of the pro-abortionists.

When the right of abortion was granted to women, the pro-choice people were immediately rewarded and have voted accordingly. I believe the people who were spared from having been aborted, the oldest of whom were born in 1973, make an interesting population to recruit to the pro-life cause. These people are alive owing only to their mother's sparing them from the abortion procedure. There are currently only about ten years' worth of voters in this classification. I wonder if these people will view abortion the same way as we older voters who were awarded the protection of the state at our conception?

I believe abortion should not be condoned by society, but it must be tolerated in order to garner enough political support to change the current law. I would wish to have abortion be unlawful, but have no consequences for the woman having the abortion. Making the procedure illegal would prohibit the government and health insurance from paying for abortions with money taken from people who are against this destruction of innocent life. It would also make the law moral. It would leave the woman with the ability to have an abortion without legal ramifications if she truly wanted one, but the law, and therefore society, would be on the side of the unborn.

# CHAPTER NINETEEN

# GUN CONTROL

In the liberal paradigm, guns are used in killings and killings are to be avoided. Therefore, if guns are outlawed, lives will be saved. In the conservative paradigm, guns do cause death, but they also prevent death. In the conservative paradigm, being armed protects people from being harmed by the lawless and by governments.

I went to high school in a growing, rural area. Because of the rapid growth, the school district chose to implement split shifts. I believe our school day started at 7:15 A.M. and ended at 12:15 P.M. Because the junior high kids were occupying the school and our coaches in the afternoon, we had several hours free prior to afternoon or early evening sports practices. I used to love to hunt, and my friends and I would often hunt after school.

In our cars parked in the high school parking lot, I'm sure we had more firepower than the murderers who shot up Columbine High School. But it would never have entered anyone's mind to use these guns against people. We learned at an early age not to point guns at anything we didn't intend to kill, and we would never have intended to kill anyone.

We lived in an area of two-lane highways, fast cars, and kids who occasionally drank. This combination led to a lot of car accidents—a lot of deadly car accidents. I knew a lot of people who died in automobile accidents. I don't know anyone who died from a gun-related cause.

If you were going to make a list of all the ways people die unnaturally, traffic accidents would outnumber all the other things on the list. Two-lane, nondivided highways are deadly. Excessive drinking and then driving is deadly. According to the Department of Transportation, there were 41,375 highway deaths in the United States in 1999. This compares to 28,874 deaths from the use of guns.

I recommend a book by John Lott, entitled *More Guns, Less Crime*, which discusses guns and the effect of different gun laws on crime statistics. After analyzing historical and regional variations in gun-control laws and crime rates, Lott concludes that guns cause deaths, but guns save more lives than they take in our society. The more restrictive the gun law in the United States, the more deaths that occur from guns. Choose the simple solution to controlling gun deaths by outlawing guns, and you will be supporting laws that will result in more deaths. Are we this heartless? Do we feel no sorrow for the victims?

Most of the time, if someone gets killed by a gun, it is a news story. If someone stops a killing with a gun, then there is no story, and the incident is therefore not reported. The news media are biased toward reporting sensational stories. There is nothing sensational about the lack of a killing.

We have so many drug-related deaths that even these are hardly news anymore. We expect it. The deaths are no longer news. Car accidents are in the same category. These deaths are expected. No news value.

Liberals argue for gun control by looking at countries that don't allow gun ownership and observing the minimal number of gun-related deaths in those countries. I believe the liberals have a point, although I am concerned that this low death rate resulting from having an unarmed populace may not always continue.

We conservatives don't trust government. Governments always have guns. When the writers of the Constitution wrote about the right to bear arms, their fear was a government that could take advantage of an unarmed populace. For a controlling government—whether fascist, communist, socialist, monarchy, or dictatorship—a basic initial requirement is to disarm the people. One of the first things the Nazis did in Germany was disarm the Jews. What was the total cost of this? At least six million deaths. Isn't this cost a bit high? Governments have been responsible for huge numbers of deaths in the past hundred years. Six million dead at the hands of the Germans, three million dead in Cambodia, twenty million dead in Ukraine, and who knows how many dead in Africa. All unarmed populaces! What are the costs to these societies of the people not being armed? The cost is unimaginable.

We conservatives view the deaths from the use of firearms as tragic, but not as tragic as the loss of being able to defend ourselves. These deaths are the total cost of allowing an armed populace. The millions killed by oppressive governments are the total cost of having an unarmed populace.

I recently watched a PBS special on the Revolutionary War. The British battle strategy was to sail across Lake Champlain and then go cross-country to the Hudson River, where they intended to proceed down the river to attack Albany. The British troops had underestimated the difficulty of this endeavor and ran out of supplies on their march from Lake Champlain to the Hudson River. To resupply the army, the British forcibly took supplies from the local people. In England, this would not have posed a problem because the population was unarmed. In America, the local population was armed and defended its property from the British. The British were soon defeated.

The use of guns as a deterrent in personal property crime is also a part of our right to defend ourselves. Law enforcement will never be 100 percent effective. Being able to protect oneself with a firearm should be a basic right for law-abiding citizens. "God created man, but Colt made them equal" is an old saying that highlights how we conservatives view the right to defend ourselves.

# CHAPTER TWENTY

# EDUCATION

In the conservative education paradigm, the desired outcome is for students to be well educated for the minimum amount of money. In the conservative paradigm, the student benefits from the education and therefore the student or the student's parents or guardians should be financially responsible for paying for the education. In the conservative paradigm, it is considered unjust to forcibly take others' money through taxation to pay for a benefit that someone else derives.

In the liberal education paradigm, education is but one goal of the school system. In the liberal paradigm, the education system is also a vehicle to promote the mixing of cultures, to foster social equalization, to provide continuing education opportunities for the adult population, to adequately educate the disabled, and to promote other various social goals. In the liberal paradigm, society as a whole benefits from having an educated populace. Therefore, society should willingly fund education because we all are better off as a result of the existence of the public schools.

In the conservative paradigm, competition causes the marketplace to produce the best product or service for the least amount of cost. This is as true for education as it is for any other endeavor. Because the government has the power to tax, the government does not need a satisfied customer to continue operating. Thus, the economic incentive to maximize the benefit gained for the least cost is lost. The market mechanism by which customers switch to a competitor if they are not happy with the quality of the product—in this case, the education provided—is also lost. The government's ability to take money forcibly has resulted in public schools that are not cost efficient and that in some cases do not do a good job of educating.

In the March 20, 2002, edition of *The Wall Street Journal* an editorial addressed the situation of the Philadelphia public school system. According to the editorial, one-third of the students drop out of school without graduating, and at the eleventh-grade level it was estimated that only 13 percent of the students had the ability to read a newspaper with any kind of comprehension. The school district's budget is $1.8 billion and it serves (if you could call it that) 204,000 students, which results in an allocation of $8,824 per student per year. In the conservative paradigm, we would like to see a vibrant, competitive educational system vying for students' education dollars. This would maximize the education benefit that each education dollar can procure.

The liberal education paradigm holds that more education is always better, and that it's impossible to spend too much on education. In the conservative paradigm, on the other hand, resources are always scarce. If resources are used for education, they will not be available for other uses such as medical care or housing. In the conservative paradigm, the consumer of scarce resources has to make decisions about where to spend the limited wealth.

In our system of government, we hope for there to be checks and balances for all things. In the marketplace, competition from other businesses is the system of checks and balances. In the public arena, the three branches of government (executive, judicial, legislative) limit the authority of each branch by establishing a system where each branch is overseen by the other branches of the government. Since public education is not a free market, the mechanism to balance the public's wishes with the school's wishes is the local school board. In the conservative paradigm the functioning of a free market will result in the best results. A system that utilizes an elected body to control education will not operate as well as a free market. Don't we owe it to the children of our society to give them the best—a free-market education consisting of educators competing for the parents or guardians of the student business?

I believe we should phase out the government operation and financing of public schools. I believe, however, that totally phasing out the public financing of education would be politically impossible. I would like to see education financed by allowing the deduction of education expenses from taxes owed, as a tax credit to poor parents, and also by charitable contributions.

# CHAPTER TWENTY-ONE

# COMPETITION TO GOVERNMENT PROGRAMS

The conservative political paradigm recognizes that an occasional government program might work, but argues that in most cases government programs produce worse results and are much more costly than equivalent nongovernment programs. Thus, it would seem to be in the best interest of taxpayers—both individual and corporate—to fund private programs that compete against government programs. Taxpayers should willingly fund the competitive entities because wealth will be saved in the long run. Let's use the government schools as an example.

Public schools are generally more costly than their private counterparts. In my own public school district, the operating budget for the 2001–2002 school year was $92,856,245, and there were 11,600 students, which calculates out to a cost of about $8,000 per pupil. This cost does not include the cost of buildings, which is included in a different budget. Tuition at private high schools in our area is about $6,500 per year, and the local parochial school's unsubsidized tuition is $2,955 per year for first through eighth grade. The taxpayers of the school district would save money if children switched to these private schools. In theory, it would seem as though the choice made by the taxpayers would be obvious. Choose the private school and save money. Even though parents have to pay the private school's tuition, the private schools are often full, resulting in no place to transfer the public school kids.

The costs mentioned here are also just the first costs. The total cost of government education is much higher in cases where the public school system provides a low-quality education. We should willingly fund student attendance at these private educational institutions because the total cost of education will decrease and the total value of the education received will increase.

Conservative politicians are currently trying to get a portion of government tax revenue made available to people to choose their own school and therefore foster competition with the government schools. I believe this private competition would be helpful, but it faces powerful political barriers. Politically, the problem with school choice initiatives is that the suburban school districts' voters—the majority of whom, I'm assuming, are conservative voters—are fairly happy with their public schools and see no reason for change. The voters in inner-city school districts—among whom, I'm assuming, liberals have the majority—are unhappy with their schools, but possibly for other reasons still vote for politicians that support the education status quo.

The forcible collection of taxes to fund education programs is unjust. I would like to see a competing private education system financed by parents, voluntary donations, and tax deductions for the parents or guardians who pay the private school tuition.

Let's say that you are in a school district that spends $8,000 per student per year. You and your fellow school district residents and businesses give $3,000 to support a student to switch to a private school that costs $6,500 per year. The student's parents agree to pay the remaining $3,500 of tuition. Your combined $3,000 donation, along with the parents' $3,500 tuition payment, saves the taxpayers of your school district $8,000, and reduces the first cost of education by a total of $1,500. Some of this money should come back to you in the future in the form of lower taxes, although it will take political effort to make sure that the government bureaucracy does not retain this savings. Some of the $3,500 in tuition paid by the parents should be returned to them in the form of a tax break. After all, the parents or guardians are unfairly paying both for the public schools through taxation and for the private school through tuition. In addition to the first-cost savings, the total cost of education will be reduced even further because the competition will improve the quality of all schools.

It would make financial sense for people and businesses to donate funds to private entities to compete with government programs because the total costs will be lower than if only the government program existed. If you know the government is going to get involved with something, it would be advantageous for people to fund the program privately. People let the government create programs they deem necessary because they cannot or will not fund desired programs themselves, and they look upon government as a means of funding the programs. The government forces everyone to pay for its programs, whether they benefit or not, so government programs are certain of getting funding. This is how our government became nine times larger than OPEC. We need to sell the taxpayers on the need to donate money to private entities. The taxpayers' donations should keep the overall size of government down and minimize future tax increases, as well as enhancing the quality of the programs.

Which of the following would you rather have take place? Would you rather be forced by threat of fines or loss of freedom to give your money to the government or would you freely give your money to non-government programs that you view as doing good? I'd rather freely give my money to the nongovernment programs.

The only problem I find with this argument is one of fairness. If you give, but others are not as charitable, is this charitable giving going to be fair to you? I answer these question two ways. First I answer the question with another question. How fair is the system now? The second is to compare the functioning of society to marriage. If you are asking the question of fairness within a marriage then the marriage is going to be headed for trouble. The real question in a marriage is if you are doing all you can do for your spouse. If both spouses view the marriage this way, then I believe marriage is great. You should not be looking for fairness, you should be looking for a good marriage. Likewise with society.

You should not be looking for fairness, but to do all that you can do. If everyone acted this way then society would be great.

I would like to see an organization formed to compete against the government sector. This competition would ensure the wise use of resources, and taxpayers could possibly be allowed to deduct the donation costs from their taxes. The funds that I would like to see established, as a minimum, are as follows:

1) Education fund

   • Primary, secondary and postsecondary school fund— to help pay tuition for students of all incomes, with a sliding scale based on the ability to pay.

   • Special education fund—to pay for physically or mentally handicapped students in private schools.

   • School building fund—to ensure that physical facilities are able to meet the rising demand for private education.

2) Environment fund—to purchase land or to fund cooperation between landowners for environmental and recreational uses.

3) Recreation fund—to pay for building recreational centers, with an emphasis on youth activities.

4) Unwanted pregnancy fund—to fund women through crisis pregnancies.

5) Library fund—to build private libraries.

6) Poor family welfare fund—to help poor families become self-sufficient.

7) Conservative legal fund—to fund legal support of conservative efforts.

Additional funds could be established to meet members' funding wishes. All of these programs would support segments of our society in which government involvement has led to suboptimal performance or excessive cost.

This new organization would require no political action to implement. Money would be needed from private sources to initiate the program, but it should save costs in the long run. As the privately funded institutions established a track record of superior performance and lower cost, political support for the government-run institutions would be undermined. Hopefully, this would lead to a less intrusive government and a government that is less than nine times the size of OPEC.

# CHAPTER TWENTY-TWO

# VICTIMIZATION

One common strategy to win votes is to convince voters that some other group is victimizing them: the majority victimizing minorities, the rich victimizing the poor, employers victimizing employees, industry victimizing the environment, the cigarette makers victimizing smokers, and on and on and on. By electing these politicians to office, you empower them to right the wrong that has been done to you and your group. It is quite easy to view yourself as a victim. Even though women outnumber men, some women have been convinced that they are a victimized minority. Perhaps women are victimized, but they are not a minority.

I'll use myself in an example of victimization. For around sixteen years, I was employed in basically the same job for a division of a fairly large corporation. Employees would come and go. Some would move up the corporate ladder and some would stay put. I could never figure out why I wasn't promoted into some area that the company deemed more important than the one I was currently in. I thought I was innovative and hard working. Why wouldn't management promote me?

I happen to be a white male, or at least a mostly white male. If I had been black, Hispanic, Asian, Native American, or some other minority, then I could have told myself that the reason I wasn't promoted was because I belonged to that particular minority. I could have been full of hate and could have contemplated suing the company for discrimination instead of trying to figure out what to do with my life. But since I wasn't a member of a minority, then that obviously could not have been the reason why I wasn't promoted.

It's very easy to talk yourself into believing that you have been victimized, in order to satisfy in your own mind the reason for someone else's decision. In most cases, however, I don't believe there's any way to tell if you are being victimized because you belong to a minority or because you lack some necessary skill or personality trait.

The people who believe they are being victimized often use statistics to show that there is indeed victimization. I think this use of statistical evidence to prove victimization can easily be abused. I'll use the National Basketball Association (NBA) as my example.

Statistically, black males dominate pro basketball in North America. If I were using statistics, then I would say that the NBA is victimizing whites. Black males are overrepresented in the NBA when compared to their numbers in the U.S. population as a whole. Do I actually believe the NBA is victimizing whites? No, it's my belief that the majority of excellent basketball players just happen to be black. People like to watch their team win, regardless of whether the team is made up of black players or white players. A basketball team owner will seek to create the best team possible because it is in the best interest of the owner. The owner could discriminate against blacks and have an all-white team, but if that team loses too many games, few fans will buy tickets. Whether the owner does or does not like black players will not affect hiring decisions. The owner wants to make money, so he or she will hire the best players possible regardless of any prejudice he or she may have.

Another example of the possible misuse of statistics to prove prejudice is the United States prison system. The U.S. Department of Justice, Bureau of Justice Statistics, maintains a Web site at www. ojp.usdoj.gov.bjs. According to the Web site there were 1,405,531 people under the jurisdiction of state or federal prison authorities in 2001. Of these prisoners only 94,336 were female. There are slightly more women than men in the United States, but less than 7 percent of the prison population is female. Should we males be claiming the judicial system is biased against males? Or do males perpetrate the vast majority of crime, which is reflected in the prison statistics? I believe the prison population rightly reflects the fact that males commit the vast majority of crime.

In my view, if a person makes irrational judgments in hiring or in commerce, the person making the irrational judgment will suffer a financial loss. The person against whom the decision has been made also suffers a loss. If this occurs, I believe it is quite unfortunate, but I don't believe the government should become involved. The total cost of bringing a legal challenge—along with the time wasted trying to comply with the laws attempting to prevent irrational decisions—is more costly than allowing the irrational decision to stand.

We live in a free economy. If you don't like what is happening to you, you are free to change where you work, where you shop, where you choose to eat, and so on. If you believe you are a victim, I think that is unfortunate, but too bad. Life isn't fair. Get over it and move on. You will be better off. For example, there have been allegations that lenders are not being fair to blacks in providing home loans. In a free market this should not happen. If I were black, and had been discriminated against, I would think about starting up a home loan company that would lend to black people. Don't get mad at the irrational decisions. Get even. If the bank won't lend to worthy applicants, then start a business that does lend to this group of worthy applicants. Free markets allow you to compete.

Our policies that make it advantageous to be part of a group based on some trait or condition have led to splintering within our society. We are no longer Americans who happen to be of Irish decent. Instead we have become Irish-Americans. The politicians try to create and take advantage of these splits. To take an extreme example, one politician who used differences in society to take political advantage was Hitler. Hitler convinced the majority of German people that the country's problems could be attributed to certain groups of people. He came to power by taking advantage of this perceived problem with certain groups of people.

In present-day America, a person's first responsibility seems in many cases to be to one of the following: his or her sexual orientation, race, previous nationality, religion, gender, political party, marital status, or labor union. This categorizing of groups of victims causes division within our country. It sets up a system to dislike other groups.

What of past wrongs done to certain groups? My advice would be to get over it. Somewhere in everyone's past, some ancestors had something done unfairly to them. The groups that dwell on past wrongs never progress. Look around the world. There are countries that are fighting battles over issues that are thousands of years old. Don't you think it's time for them to move on? At the other extreme are the relationships between Japan, Germany, and the United States. We fought a huge war against these people. Do you think we still hold each other in contempt for the past? I don't believe we do. These countries have improved their standards of living by moving on with life.

Racial profiling has recently become a big issue. Racial profiling is when law enforcement departments target certain groups for a high level of scrutiny. A recent example of this profiling is the tight scrutiny of people at airports who look like they may be from the Middle East. I don't believe it should be a policy of any government agency to select certain segments of our society for more law enforcement surveillance, nor do I believe that any law enforcement agency makes a practice of profiling any particular group as a matter of policy. On the other hand, law enforcement people need to be allowed to do their jobs based on their personal experiences or known facts. I don't want the police in my area stopping elderly women at the same rate they stop young males. I don't want elderly women who are citizens to be subject to the same level of suspicion as noncitizen young males at the airport. However, if elderly women suddenly start being a major contributor to crime or terrorism, then I would want the police to react accordingly. We expect our law enforcement agencies to protect us. I would hope that law enforcement personnel would be able to use their experience and knowledge to accomplish the goal of keeping the populace safe.

CHAPTER TWENTY-THREE

# DYSFUNCTION

There are a number of reasons why dysfunctional behavior is included in this writing about politics. One of the reasons is because you have to be able to sense when the political discussion is no longer rational. Logic won't take you there. If logic doesn't win, it may not be because your logic was wrong; the problem might be that logic isn't driving the system.

I have the common male affliction of being a television station surfer. I don't like to watch one show at a time. Once, while watching a Sunday football game, I clicked through the stations during a commercial break. I ended up watching a PBS program with John Bradshaw discussing dysfunctional behavior. I know this may sound like some pop psychology book, but please bear with me. The information presented by Bradshaw was a paradigm shift for me. Bradshaw has written extensively on this subject, and I would recommend any of his works relating to dysfunction in the family.

Bradshaw had an explanation as to why people behave in irrational, oftentimes harmful ways. He explained that emotional development takes place prior to logical development. If emotional development does not take place correctly owing to some kind of emotional trauma, you may make some very irrational, damaging behavioral decisions throughout your life, trying to meet some emotional need.

My own definition of dysfunction is that something other than God becomes your god. Dysfunction takes all kinds of shapes and forms. To substance abusers, the substance becomes their god. To workaholics, work becomes their god. To people who value success over everything else, money or power becomes their god. To people who need emotional control over others, control becomes their god. Even religion can become your god.

I think dysfunction is quite common. If you are from a functional family and have always dealt with mostly functional people, then you might have difficulty grasping this concept. In my view, dysfunction is a very real phenomenon, and it drives a large number of social and political situations.

To the functional, the actions of the dysfunctional may appear to be stupid. People ask, "Why would a person do something so foolish?"

It reminds me of the old story of the man who had a flat tire in front of an insane asylum. While changing the tire, the man accidentally drops the lug nuts down a sewer grate. He mutters to himself, wondering what to do now that the lug nuts are out of reach below the grate. One of the inmates of the insane asylum overhears his muttering and suggests that he remove a lug nut from each of the remaining wheels to fasten the changed tire to the car until he can get additional parts. The man changing the tire looks at the inmate and says, "That's a pretty good idea. With that much intelligence, why are you in the insane asylum?" The inmate replies that he is in the asylum because he is crazy, not because he is stupid.

I believe that many political people—like many outwardly successful people in other fields—are dysfunctional. These dysfunctional people have an overwhelming desire to look publicly successful, even though their private lives may be in ruins. Many politicians need the political position to meet their emotional need of looking important and successful to the public.

In my opinion, President Clinton was a classic example of dysfunction. I'm not going to pick on just President Clinton; we'll get to the

Republicans in a minute. When President Clinton's supporters found out that he was having at least some kind of relationship with a White House intern, I often heard his supporters ask, "How could such a gifted man do such a stupid thing?" My answer to this question is that it was a dysfunctional act, not a stupid act.

President Clinton's approval ratings were high even though he was both caught in a lie and caught doing things that we would not find acceptable behavior on the part of anyone with whom we had a personal relationship. Why? I think it was because he had a winning public persona. He was a great politician, if you define political greatness in terms of being successful in manipulating public opinion and in terms of winning elections.

Clinton, who was the leader of our country at the time, was caught in a number of lies. He fought the impeachment charges instead of doing the honorable thing and resigning. A classic dysfunctional behavior took place after the impeachment trial was over and he had escaped removal from office. The first thing he thought about was not his behavior, but how he was going to get even with the House of Representatives' managers and Linda Tripp. There was no sense of shame, no sense of honor. The shame would have been in losing. I can just picture him plotting his revenge. This was truly a case of an emotional five-year-old in the body of a politically powerful man.

An example of political dysfunction operating on a larger scale can be seen in the comparison of Presidents Nixon and Clinton. For younger readers who do not remember Richard Nixon, let me give you a little background. Nixon was a Republican president in the late 60s and early 70s. He was caught trying to cover up a break-in at a Democratic political office (in the Watergate Hotel) by a person hired by a Republican strategist. Nixon was charged with trying to cover up the crime and resigned from office prior to certain impeachment and forcible removal from office.

I look at the different outcomes of the Clinton and Nixon presidencies, and the differences I see in the two situations are not the differences between the two men, whom I believe were both dysfunctional, but in the emotional makeup of their parties' political leaders. The political backers of

Nixon, once they found out what was going on, immediately abandoned him. In contrast, the Clinton backers who became aware of what Clinton was all about became even stronger backers. The dysfunctional support the person regardless of what he or she has done, because the dysfunctional person is one of their own. The functional look at the person, regardless of whom he or she may be, and judge the person based on his or her actions. Nixon resigned, with little support from the conservative leadership. The dysfunctional Nixon retired in disgrace, forced out of office by his own people. Clinton remained in office with almost the full support of the liberal leadership. The dysfunctional Clinton was celebrated, and his wife ran for and won a high political office. As a casual observer of human behavior, I find this comparison fascinating.

Dysfunction is found in some groups that end up with political clout that is way out of proportion with their numbers. Because these people are driven by an emotional need, they can harness great energy for something that the functional may not feel is worth fighting over. The functional have balanced lives, with commitments that do not allow them to devote the same level of time or energy that the dysfunctional can contribute to their agenda. The functional have lives. The dysfunctional have causes. The functional highly value their personal relationships and recognize that there is a cost to keeping these relationships working. The dysfunctional easily let relationships lapse in order to fulfill some other overriding emotional need.

Bradshaw's depiction of dysfunctional behavior is when people will do actual harm to themselves to fulfill an emotional need. I look at inner-city voters in this light. Inner-city schools are dismal failures, yet the voters in these inner cities support liberal political candidates who are the greatest defenders of government education and the government education establishment. Not having a better school system really harms these voters' children. If there is logic in this I fail to see it. Hopefully it is not dysfunction that is the problem in these areas, but simply the conservatives' poor job of selling their message.

It may be nearly impossible to change dysfunctional behavior. To the dysfunctional, dysfunction is normal. I have seen dysfunction operating in work situations. For example, some people cannot tolerate not having tension in the workplace. Tension, for them, is a normal part of life. Not having tension is uncomfortable. These people create tension in order to have a feeling of normality. If you are unlucky enough to have a boss who is this way, it can be very unpleasant.

The only way the dysfunctional can change is to rely on the functional to inform them of the truth, or to examine their lives and realize that something is amiss. This is quite difficult, which is why most people do not change. You have to rely on someone else to tell you what the reality is, and not trust your own judgment. A substance abuser, for example, must realize that not everyone ends up with all the problems that he or she has. Substance abusers don't always reach this point, even though the substance abuse is causing them much physical and mental anguish. What chance is there, then, to change a person's mindset when it comes to a less life-impacting situation such as politics? I hope the conservative politician will recognize the difficulty of changing people's minds and not become discouraged. It may not be the message that is the problem, but the willingness of the listener to hear the message.

# CHAPTER TWENTY-FOUR

# BEING PASSIONATE ABOUT CONSERVATISM

There are two inherent problems with conservatives and the operation of government. First, because of the conservative belief that the government does not solve problems and that unnecessary government actually creates problems, there is little or no conservative participation in what is viewed as unnecessary government. Thus, non-conservatives tend to dominate these sectors of government. Liberals love government and believe in its capacity to do good, so it's easy to find liberals willing to fill virtually any government position—whether necessary or unnecessary. The solution to this first problem is for conservatives to get passionate about the good that can come from shrinking the size and influence of government, and to get themselves into positions where they can work toward the shrinking of government.

The second problem is that national politicians are expected to bring federal money back to their particular state or congressional district. If a conservative is elected and does not partake in this federal spoils system, the constituents of the conservative politician in aggregate will suffer financially and the voters may not send the elected official back to Washington.

I cannot stress enough the proposal in chapter nine of this book to amend the Sixteenth Amendment. The job of elected officials should be the management of a limited amount of government tax revenue to fund necessary government, not redistribution of an unlimited amount of government tax revenue. Our conservative representatives should stress that they want to minimize government through a change to the Sixteenth Amendment, but that they are not going to commit political suicide by letting their liberal opponents play Santa Claus to their constituents while the conservatives play the role of Scrooge to their constituents.

The conservative paradigm will always recognize the many benefits of limited government, but it also has to recognize that in our present system, where the courts have abandoned individual economic freedom to the tyranny of the majority, the only way to institute a system of limited government is through the election process. As conservatives, we have to actively pursue the recruiting of non-conservative voters and non-voters to our conservative paradigm in order to gain enough political power to institute a system of limited government.

How do we go about this recruiting process? Unfortunately, the conservative paradigm is not the prevailing paradigm, so we try to persuade and educate our political opponents as part of our political discussion. When we explain our conservative position, we stumble into trying to explain the position from within the liberal paradigm. We come across as apologetic, unsure of ourselves and of our conservative positions. We need to show confidence and debate as if the conservative paradigm were the norm.

If you are already a conservative, rationally argue with our political opponents that many critical issues—retirement, health care, education, helping the poor—are all issues much too important to entrust to the government.

If you are already a conservative, use the tools of total cost and fractional experimentation to help convince others of the beauty of small but competent government. Argue the need for an enforced Constitution and a shift of power away from the federal government to the states.

This will enable experimentation and competition between the states to optimize the function of government.

As I said at the beginning of this book, conservatives and liberals want basically the same things—prosperity and peace. I think even many non-conservatives recognize that our society has problems that additional taxation and government involvement won't solve. It's time to try the opposite approach and give conservatism a chance.

If you are not a conservative, I invite you to adopt the conservative political paradigm and help free everyone—poor, middle class, and rich—from oppressive government, and in doing so raise the standard of living, especially the standard of living of the poor and the middle class.

Adopt the conservative paradigm and strengthen our national defense and local law enforcement.

Adopt the conservative paradigm and free the poor from the dead-end path of socialism, with the moral and economic decay that inevitably results from government dependency.

Adopt the conservative paradigm and join the fight against the forcible taking of our money through the specific taxation that is transferred to others—money taken in the name of helping the poor, but which ultimately ends up being consumed by the government bureaucracy and given to the non-poor. The poor are even forced to pay taxes on their meager wages, sometimes—as in the case of Social Security taxes—only to have these funds redistributed to people who are actually much better off.

Our health care system is expensive and not optimized. People die unnecessarily every day because of bureaucratic delays in implementing new drugs and equipment. The problem is that people never think of these deaths as being caused by bureaucracy because they do not know that there are new treatments available to prevent the deaths. You are not aware of what you don't know. Join with the conservatives to help save these people. The life you may be saving could be your own or that of someone you love.

Join the conservative cause and call for an end to government confiscation of private property. In the name of the environment, people's land is, for all intents and purposes, taken from them without government reimbursement. In the name of the environment, the government has put farmers and loggers out of business or out of work without compensation, while society as a whole does not share the financial burden of this government action.

The government restricts the availability of land for housing by owning huge amounts of land and implementing building restrictions to reduce urban sprawl. These restrictions drive up the price of land, which in turn drives up the price of housing, making it unaffordable for the poor. Help us right this wrong.

Help our families who are hit with huge tax burdens that bring incredible financial strain to the already fragile institution of family. Wouldn't it be wonderful if taxes were no longer the largest expense for most families? Join us in eliminating hidden taxes, so that the people can judge if government spending is out of control. Reveal the taxes that are forced on employers and that damage vital employer/employee relationships. Help us enable businesses to create jobs in the appealing middle class and upper-middle class income levels that may be disappearing because of the high marginal tax burden placed on wages in these salary ranges.

Help us enable poor children, who want to help their families out financially, to take meaningful jobs, diminishing the temptation to seek employment in illegal enterprises. Help these same poor children to become better educated by establishing a free market for education and replacing the bureaucratic government school establishment.

Help us to delegitimize the morally corrupt abortion procedure that takes place partly with the financial backing of people who are steadfastly against this destruction of innocent human life.

Join me in trying to right these wrongs. Join me in donating to causes that we know to be just. Join me in trying to increase the number of people within the conservative paradigm. Join me in the spirit of Robin Hood to work against a government whose size has grown to be nine times the size of OPEC at the expense of the people. Join with me and other like-minded conservatives by participating in the group I am establishing, called the Robin Hood Republican[SM] voters.

This conservative effort is in its infancy, but I sense a great wish on the part of freedom-loving people to partake in such a cause. The grouping of non-conservatives and conservatives under one political label leads to conservatives not only having to deal with non-conservatives from other parties, but also having to deal with the non-conservatives within our own party. To have a political subset of conservatives advancing the conservative viewpoint will help in this effort to reduce the impact of government. The subset will identify those who share our political philosophy while maintaining the big tent strategy of accepting non-conservatives who share some, but not all of our conservative values.

I have a domain name: (http://robinhoodrepublican.com) and information may be located at the Web site as this effort expands. If this effort is successful, information will also be made available through traditional media outlets.

To initiate and maintain competition with government programs is going to take financial support. This may be a financial burden for you. Please keep in mind that a financial burden now should reduce your future tax burden and increase your level of freedom. I would personally like this effort to start with education. The funding level I suggest starting with is to voluntarily donate an amount equal to one-fourth of your current property taxes. The structure to accept this money is not yet in place, but try to come up with a financial strategy that would allow you to contribute at this rate once the programs are up and running.

In the interim, please inform like-minded people of this effort and pursue changing the minds of the other-minded people. If this book helps in that cause, then by all means pass it along. If each person who agrees with this philosophy seeks out ten others and this process of seeking ten others is repeated four times then we have 10,000 people contacted. If this process is repeated six times, then we have a million people contacted, and if this process is repeated ten times we have contacted every citizen of the United States more than three times.

This effort will need to take place at a grassroots level and depends on each and every person who agrees with this philosophy to spread the message. I'm assuming this effort will not be supported by most of the major media outlets, the powers that be in most of the major political organizations, most big businesses, and the supporters and participants of big government. I am always impressed with the creativity of people. Please take a minute and see if you can come up with a creative way of furthering this cause.

The existence of the Internet could make the dissemination of this information a relatively simple task. If you agree with most of this book's message and you would want to further spread this information, please take a minute to write a short note and forward this note to everyone in your Internet address book that that you are comfortable contacting about this subject matter. Also, if you personally know people that would be sympathetic to our cause in positions (broadcast and print media personalities, political and religious leaders) who are able to reach many people, please inform them of this effort.

I stated at the start of this book that I oftentimes entered into political conversations with non-conservatives. My initial reason for writing this book was to fully explain my political philosophy to these people, an endeavor that cannot adequately take place in a hallway political discussion. My first two copies of this book will be given as gifts to two past coworkers who also happened to be political adversaries and hopefully who will still be friends after reading this. Hopefully they will become conservative friends. If you have similar non-conservative political acquaintances, this book may be the perfect gift.

The book may be purchased online as either a single copy or in the much less expensive bulk order quantities through www. MidwestBookHouse.com. The ISBN number (1931646538) may also be used to order the book through your local bookstore. The book should also be available from other popular online outlets. If this ordering information changes, I will put the updated information on the Robin Hood Republican[SM] voter's Web site (http://robinhoodrepublican.com).

Thank you for taking the time to read this book. My hope is that the reading of this book was a thought-provoking endeavor. My further hope is that this book will be the catalyst for you to become more politically involved and will supply both you and others with explainable reasons for being rationally right.

# APPENDIX

2001 Federal Government Budget and Expenditures
(From www.whitehouse.gov/omb/budget/fy2003/bud34.html)

| 2001 REVENUES (FROM TABLE S-11; RECEIPTS BY SOURCE, STATED IN BILLIONS OF DOLLARS) | |
|---|---|
| Individual income taxes | 994.3 |
| Social insurance and retirement receipts | 694.0 |
| Corporate income taxes | 151.1 |
| Excise taxes | 66.1 |
| Estate tax and gift tax | 28.4 |
| Customs duties | 19.4 |
| Miscellaneous | 37.8 |
| Total | 1,991.5 |

| 2001 EXPENDITURES (FROM TABLE S-13; OUTPLAY TOTALS BY FUNCTION, IN BILLIONS OF DOLLARS) | |
|---|---|
| Social Security | 433.1 |
| National defense | 308.5 |
| Income security | 269.8 |
| Medicare | 217.5 |
| Interest on the debt | 206.2 |
| Health | 172.6 |
| Education training, employment, and social services | 57.3 |
| Transportation | 55.2 |
| Veterans benefits and service | 45.8 |
| Administration of justice | 30.4 |
| Agriculture | 26.6 |
| Natural resources and the environment | 26.3 |
| General science, space, and technology | 19.9 |
| International affairs | 16.6 |
| General government | 15.2 |
| Community and regional development | 12.0 |
| Commerce and housing credit | 6.0 |
| Energy | 0.1 |
| Subtotal | 1,991.0 |
| Undistributed offsetting receipts | -55.2 |
| Total | 1,863.9 |